Yesterday's Cincinnati

Seemann's Historic Cities Series

LUKE FECK

Yesterday's CINCINNATI

Seemann's Historic Cities Series No. 19

E. A. Seemann Publishing, Inc.
Miami, Florida

Library of Congress Cataloging in Publication Data

Feck, Luke.
    Yesterday's Cincinnati.

    (Seemann's historic cities series ; no. 19)
    SUMMARY: Brief text and numerous historical photo-
graphs, engravings, drawings, woodcuts, etc., trace
Cincinnati's history from first settlement to the early
1950's.
    1. Cincinnati--History--Pictorial works.
2. Cincinnati--Description--Views. [1. Cincinnati--
History--Pictorial works. 2. Cincinnati--Description--
Views] I. Title.
F499.C5F43   977.1'78'00222   75-14411
ISBN 0-912458-59-3

First paperback edition, 1977

Copyright © 1975 by Luke Feck
Library of Congress Catalog Card Number: 75-14411
ISBN 0-912458-91-7

Manufactured in the United States of America

Contents

Preface

SPECIAL THANKS are due those who helped prepare this affectionate glance at Cincinnati. Obviously photographers, both amateur and professional, are key to a project of this sort. With lens aimed and focused on an event, they are often the unappreciated historians. My appreciation.

The bulk of the pictures in this book came from the files of *The Cincinnati Enquirer.* It is a tribute to *Enquirer* librarian Fred Morgener that so many pictures so rich in value can be found so readily. Important photos also were supplied by *The Cincinnati Post* library.

The Cincinnati Historical Society's unequalled picture collection filled many photographic gaps. Stephen Starr's staff was most helpful. The Cincinnati Public Library also supplied certain photographs.

Much of the background came from books about Cincinnati, especially Charles Cist's "Cincinnati in 1841," "Sketches and Statistics of Cincinnati in 1851" and D.J. Kenny's "Illustrated Guide to Cincinnati." Three books of special value were Iola Hessler's "Cincinnati Then and Now," Mable Morsbach's "We Live in Cincinnati" and the exceptional Ohio Writers' Project, "Cincinnati Guide."

Thanks to all four sets of my great grandparents who discovered Cincinnati variously between the 1830s and 1850s. Finally, profound thanks and appreciation to my wife, Gail, whose help was beyond measure and certainly beyond the call of the marriage vows.

CINCINNATI IN 1802 was firmly planted in the first plain up from the river. In the right background is Fort Washington. Martin Baum and Griffin Yeatman were neighbors across Sycamore Street, the second street from the right, while Israel Ludlow and Colonel Gibson lived across from each other on Main Street.

1788: A Queen Is Born

MRS. TROLLOPE thought Cincinnati was a municipal pig sty. But Charles Dickens, just a few years later, found young Cincinnati a lovely town. William Wadsworth Longfellow wrote of "The Queen City" and Winston Churchill thought Cincinnati was one of America's most beautiful inland cities. It took a long time for Cincinnati to evolve and make its impression on people. From its earliest time, the river was the thread running through the civic tapestry.

During prehistoric times what is now called the Ohio River flowed up the Little Miami River out Duck Creek Road, before most of that became highway I-71, and up toward Hamilton. It came back down part of the Great Miami River bed. The Licking River flowed on up the Millcreek Valley. There was a large lake over the Cincinnati basin (or at least a high backwater), and a natural barrier across the Ohio around Anderson Ferry.

The Ice Age pulverized the Cincinnati area topography, making hills and fossil troves, and sticking the river back about where it should be—to a point where you would recognize it.

Once the geography settled down, a band of so-called Indians settled the area around the time of Christ's birth. They were known as the Moundbuilders, but where they came from nobody knows. Artifacts from that era are still visible, along with the mounds themselves, near North Bend and at Fort Ancient near Lebanon. Mounds, used for burials, ceremonies, and defense have also been found in what is now downtown Cincinnati (Mound Street), in Sayler Park, and near Turpin Hills. Serpent Mound in Adams County to the east is more than one thousand feet long and looks like a snake with an egg in its mouth.

The last of the Moundbuilders disappeared from this area about the same time Jamestown, Virginia, was colonized. Southwestern Ohio had no established Indian

[9]

SOLDIERS from an earlier time drill outside Fort Washington.

tribes when the Indians along the Atlantic coast were seeing the first hordes of colonists.

By 1669 Robert de La Salle was rowing past the future site of Cincinnati. He called the river "La Belle Riviere" or Beautiful River. Indians who hunted here called it "Oh-he-yo" or Great River.

Hunting was easy. Indians who migrated here were primarily losers. They were Erie Indians shoved west by Iroquois who had been pushed out by the colonists. Later, Seneca, Miami, Shawnee, Ottawa, Delaware, and Wyandot tribes moved into Ohio, and the southwest corner began to have that lived-in look.

In 1778 nearly eighty men, serving the governor of Virginia, came upstream from New Orleans with a cargo of guns. They were attacked and defeated by five hundred Indians led by Simon Girty, the renegade terror of the area. One of the few survivors of that first Indian fight was Robert Benham, who later had the first sawed-log cabin in Cincinnati and ran the ferry to Newport.

In 1784 the Northwest Territory was created. It included all the land above the Ohio, east of the Mississippi, and south of the Great Lakes. The area was to contain not more than five states, slavery was prohibited, and the Indians, settlers were assured, would move away. But no one told the Indians!

The land between the Miami Rivers, the site discovered by Revolutionary War Major Benjamin Stites and acquired by Judge John Cleves Symmes, was called the Miami Slaughterhouse because of the Indian fights. Stites first explored the area when he followed Indian horse thieves across the Ohio at the mouth of the Little Miami River. Impressed by the land's fertility and the abundance of game, he came away ready to be the territory's first real estate speculator. He met Judge Symmes in New York, where Congress was in session. The judge took an inspection trip the next year and Symmes Purchase was the result. The area was one million acres, almost all of present Hamilton County and more. The land sold to all comers for sixty-six and two-thirds cents an acre. Later the price went to a dollar. Symmes had paid sixteen and two-thirds cents an acre.

Cincinnati's time was coming. Benjamin Stites acquired about ten thousand acres right where he first walked at the mouth of the Little Miami.

On November 18, 1788, twenty-six persons including four women and two children pulled their flatboats out of the river and founded the community of Columbia near the present site of Lunken Airport. By 1790 there were fifty homes. The fields of Turkey Bottom were in crops. But the Ohio River in flood tide threatened the young community.

Matthias Denman, owner of 8,000 acres opposite the Licking, brought in a team of surveyors. One of them, John Filson, came up with the classic name of L-os-anti-ville, meaning the town opposite the mouth of L(icking) River. Surveyor-linguist Filson disappeared into the woods one day. The Miami Slaughterhouse had claimed another victim.

It was four days after Christmas, 1788, when the first inhabitants arrived at Losantiville. There were no women or children at Yeatman's Cove, now the foot of Sycamore Street; but there was plenty of cold, and the settlers were a good high plain away from rampaging flood water.

Two months later—in February 1789—Judge Symmes arrived in the area. He had passed Columbia, where some cabins stood in water. Losantiville appeared to be high and dry, but the judge wanted the place with the northernmost sweep in the river, near where the Great Miami flows into the Ohio. At North Bend, Symmes established the town he felt sure would be the hub of the Northwest Territory.

Indian raids bothered settlers in all three towns and a few outlying communities such as Covalt Station in Terrace Park and Dunlap Station in what is now Colerain Township. The government promised protection in the form of a fort to be built somewhere in Symmes Purchase. When surveyors arrived, Columbia was under water. So was North Bend. Losantiville was selected as the site of Fort Washington be-

[11]

PIONEERS' LANDING at Yeatman's Cove at the foot of what would be Sycamore Street on December 28, 1788 marks the beginning of Cincinnati.

THE YOUNG CITY sprawled slightly by the decade of 1810-1820. Steamboats began to dot the river landing.

cause the river was tamer there. The new fort protected the village, which grew and prospered as the needs of its 300 soldiers gave employment opportunities for early settlers. Designed for 1500 men, the fort stood near the present Lytle Park.

The new fort was soon inspected by the governor of the Northwest Territory, General Arthur St. Clair. Not a classicist, St. Clair decided that Losantiville was a rather pretentious name for the village and he renamed it Cincinnati after the Revolutionary War officers' Society of the Cincinnati. (Cincinnatus was a Roman farmer who was drafted, led an army to victory, and after the battle beat his sword into a plow.)

Semantic problems solved, St. Clair and General Josiah Harmar chose to attack the obstreperous Indians. Harmar marched out an Indian trail, now Reading Road, and eventually lost to the Indians at Fort Wayne on October 21, 1790. The next year General St. Clair himself went to do battle and lost 900 men on the banks of the Wabash. The November defeat demoralized residents of the tiny Ohio village. Some headed back east, others moved across the river to Kentucky. Two years later, General "Mad Anthony" Wayne and his trained Indian fighters marched out what was to become Central Parkway, to the fateful Battle of Fallen Timbers, near Toledo.

Victory at Fallen Timbers brought the Treaty of Greenville, ending the Indian menace and allowed full farming, hunting, and commerce throughout the area to get underway. The need for Fort Washington diminished. It was abandoned in 1803 and destroyed in 1808.

The river in those early years was Cincinnati's focus. Early pioneers came downstream on flatboats loaded with personal items, livestock, seed, and looms. When the boats arrived they were often dismantled and the lumber was used to build cabins.

[12]

IF CINCINNATI has a claim on John James Audubon, it is that he got his vision of "the elephant folio" while living here on East Third Street. The elephant folio was to be a limited edition book of North American fowl drawn and painted to size. Audubon left his family to shift for itself in October of 1820 when he headed downriver in a flatboat tracking the migrating birds. The man, who now represents protection of birds and wildlife, was an expert hunter and his diary reports his exploits in shooting birds. He died in 1851, unaware of the movement he had begun.

Later keelboats took over the river with a singular advantage: not only could they float downriver, they could be propelled upstream against the current, as well. But even the keelboats and colorful crewmen like Mike Fink were doomed.

In 1811 the steamboat *New Orleans* came round the bend and into view of the Public Landing, launching the riverboat era that saw Cincinnati grow faster than any inland city and prosper as no one dreamed.

Eventually the city would build a steamboat a week, but not until the 1870s. The first steamboat built at Cincinnati was *The Vista. Natchez,* called the fastest steamboat on the river, was built here, too. One of the early steamboats gave the name of a state to each of the rooms. From then on, "stateroom" was a commonly used term.

The landing rang with the voices of the roustabouts. Early visitors came away with the impression of vitality and song along the riverfront. Stephen Foster, who was working for his brother on Front Street, went often to the river for inspiration. "Oh, Susannah" was one of the more famous songs he wrote here.

The levee boomed. As many as ten or twenty steamboats would await a landing at the place referred to as "Ragtown" because of the amount of rags used here by early paper manufacturers. The city was so dominant that rivermen called the Ohio the Cincinnati River. From Ragtown on the Cincinnati River, produce and pork, paper and furniture spread through the heartland of America. Cincinnati was growing: husky, healthy, happy.

New impetus came in 1827 with the opening of the first leg of the Miami and Erie Canal from Cincinnati to Dayton. Later the canal connected with Lake Erie at To-

THE ARCHDIOCESE OF CINCINNATI began officially in 1821. Father Edward Fenwick, later a bishop, is said to have celebrated the first mass in Cincinnati in 1814. The first Catholic church was built in 1819 at the corner of Vine and Liberty streets just outside the city limits where the land was so much cheaper. Two years later, Bishop Fenwick established the Diocese of Cincinnati.

ledo. Markets in central Ohio and later Pennsylvania and New York were made accessible. For those who wanted to trade with the South, Cincinnati had become the gateway. The canal was a landmark until the railroads took over. But by 1885 people were calling the canal a cesspool and demanding that it be closed. In 1920 it was dug out for a subway. Eventually Central Parkway was routed right where the canal was, but the subway—still there—was never put to use.

The flood of 1832 all but ruined Cincinnati's commercial district, which was under water for days. Just after the flood water receded, a sick passenger disembarked from a steamboat and cholera struck the crowded community. More than 800 died, and the Cincinnati Orphan Asylum was founded to take care of the children who had survived their parents. Then, fire in the downtown area burned out almost a full block of buildings.

Early farmers around Cincinnati found that corn thrived in this soil, in this climate. But getting the corn to market presented a problem. Canny farmers decided to send their corn to market on pigs' feet, and thus began one of Cincinnati's largest early industries—meat packing.

Cincinnati had so many pigs wandering the streets downtown that it was soon derisively but profitably called Porkopolis. If Chicago was to become the hog butcher of the world, it was only after wresting that crown from the Queen City. Visitors marveled that their carriages were stopped to permit pigs to be herded across the street. Stray animals roamed the streets eating garbage and spreading disease, perhaps including the dread cholera, which struck again in 1848, killing as many as one-hundred a day for six weeks. So many slaughterhouses were situated along Deer Creek that its waters ran red from the butchering. In 1841, way out in the country (near Brighton), one meat packing plant put in lights so work could go on round the clock. Huge caverns underground were filled with ice hauled in by canal, insuring that the meat was cool and better preserved.

Industrial development of by-products was intense and extensive. Fat from the slaughterhouses was used in the manufacture of soap and candles, previously home-made. Barrels were needed to ship salt pork. Hides were used to make shoes, harnesses, and saddles. Wagons, carriages, and carts were built here. Machinery shipped from Cincinnati spurred manufacturers elsewhere. Spinning machines and lathes, printing presses and flour mills moved to all parts of the country from the Public Landing.

And the factories needed workers. By 1840 there were 35,000 more people in the town than in 1820. By the start of the Civil War, Cincinnati had more than tripled its population to 161,044. Twenty years after that, 250,000 people lived here, and Cincinnati was the sixth-largest city in America.

The first large influx from overseas brought the Germans, who began to arrive here in the 1830s. The Ohio River Valley reminded them of the Rhine Valley back home. Early Germans were encouraged by Nicholas Longworth to help him grow grapes on Mount Adams for his thriving wine business, and Cincinnati became for a time the wine center of the country. The word sped back to the revolution-troubled homeland, and increasing numbers of Germans headed for Cincinnati, more than thirty thousand in all. The Miami Canal became their Rhine, and the place where the Germans lived was "Over the Rhine." Said D. J. Kenny in *Illustrated Cincinnati:*

"One has no sooner entered the northern districts of the city lying beyond Court Street across the canal, than he finds himself in another atmosphere—a foreign land.

[15]

FOURTH STREET west of Vine looked prosperous in 1837. Reuben Springer lived next to the Presbyterian Church, and Dr. Daniel Drake's office was across the street.

The people are Germans; their very gossip is German. They cook their food by German recipes, and sit long over their foaming beer, ever and again shaking it 'round their glass with that peculiar motion which none but a German can impart to the beverage he loves. There is less positive crime, less disposition to rioting and drunkenness among the beer-loving Transrhenanes than in almost every other district of any other city in the land."

By 1841, 28 percent of the city was German. The Germans loved their work, their beer, their music, and their exercise. They had their first "saengerfest" in 1849. By 1873, three dozen musical societies combined to present a huge festival of song in Saengerhall for the first May Festival, still a flourishing tradition. By 1878, Music Hall, the gift of Reuben Springer, was built to house the festival in the Over-the-Rhine area.

The Germans' interest in exercise resulted in Cincinnati's schools having one of the earliest and biggest physical education programs in America.

A potato famine in Ireland at the start of the 1840s brought many Irish to Cincinnati. Industrious and diligent, the Irish made their homes along the river, where there was usually construction work available. They put much of the brawn into Cincinnati's canals, railroads, and houses. Eventually the Irish moved from the riverside and spread throughout the city.

More than sixty-six hundred blacks lived in and around Cincinnati by 1850. Jobs on the river as roustabouts and mechanics were plentiful, and one historian felt that blacks had more economic opportunity in Cincinnati than in any other city before 1860. Cincinnati was the first free stop in the Underground Railroad, but most escaping slaves chose to continue north into Canada.

Cincinnati was in a unique spot geographically and philosophically. Many of its major markets were in the slave-holding states. Many of its citizens were proslavery, and others were vehement abolitionists. Harriet Beecher Stowe, daughter of Lyman Beecher, the first head of Lane Seminary in Walnut Hills, based *Uncle Tom's Cabin* on many of her Cincinnati experiences, and the book played a large role in inflaming the passions that made the Civil War such a bitter struggle. Throughout that period in Cincinnati there was debate and violence over the slavery issue. The shop of abolitionist printer Achilles Pugh was wrecked twice by angry proslavery mobs.

So stood Cincinnati, poised, not so polished, certainly not ready for the trauma of the Civil War. Charles Cist described Cincinnati's growth from its early days in *Cincinnati in 1851*:

PORKOPOLIS: Pig butchering started Cincinnati's climb to nineteenth-century prominence.

WILLIAM PROCTER (left), candle molder, and James Gamble, soap boiler, married sisters before starting a business in 1837. The first Procter and Gamble firm was at Sixth and Main streets, where its former home office, the Gwynne Building, still stands. The plant moved to Central Avenue, and in 1885 to Ivorydale.

"A few scattered settlements—a military post here and there—two or three small villages, of which this was one, surrounded by hostile savages, were all the lodgments which the white man had then made, in this now mighty region of the west . . . ."

And in 1810 "Comforts were provided under the instincts of necessity; the church, the school, the court-house, and the road, each appeared in its turn, and, having overcome the hardships of pioneer life, glowing accounts go back of happy western homes . . . . An infant commerce has sprung up, which was floated on the ark, the keel, and the barge . . . . The genius of Bolton and Watt, had evolved the new motive power of steam . . . .

"Another decade (1820s), where were we then? This is the period which dates an era. The magic influence of steam had been felt and everywhere acknowledged. New life, new energy, new hope, new vitality, new action, were everywhere visible. The settlements were no longer isolated. There was the mill, the factory, the forge . . . . We had subdued the rivers and lakes, and made them subservient to our will . . . .

"Let us come down another period, and then look. Twenty years ago—ah! there is the stagecoach and the ponderous Conestoga wagon, rolling over the scientifically built turnpike; there waves the rich harvest in the west where the forest waved ten years before; there rises the stately mansion, where the primitive cabin stood; there the opulent city, once the village site; and mark the fleets of noble steamers, which swarm our lakes and rivers.

"Ten years ago—and where? why, we had risen to the rank of a mighty people, doubling in number . . . . Our voice was heard with attention in the halls of national legislation. The tide of emigration . . . . had now swollen and was rolling towards us in a mighty volume . . . . Our giant strides had astonished our eastern brethren . . . . Turnpikes and canals were stretched out towards us, from all directions . . . ."

MRS. FRANCES TROLLOPE did not like Cincinnati in the late 1820s. A proper Englishwoman, she arrived here and eventually built her Bazaar on East Third Street. Mrs. Trollope was unable to pay for the strange structure and was forced to return to England where she wrote her acrid *Domestic Manners of the Americans,* which took Americans in general and Cincinnatians in particular to task. The building was taken over by Ohio Mechanic's Institute which used the cupola of the bizarre Bazaar as an ornate fire tower. Cincinnati's famed expositions of the 1870-80s grew from OMI expositions. OMI is now part of the University of Cincinnati.

Cist concluded that the decade ending in 1860 would be noted for the telegraph and the railroad, and he called the railroad "the great disturbing cause (which) must settle and determine the destiny and relative position of various cities or centres, which are struggling for supreme ascendency on this continent."

Cist was partly right. The city on the edge of the Civil War would never be the same. Other cities would catch up and would pass her. Cincinnati would become more introspective. It was still vital and brawny but somehow very, very different.

WILLIAM HENRY HARRISON'S campaign for president was colorful and successful. His North Bend home overlooked the Whitewater Canal and the Ohio River in the foreground. Harrison, one-time commander at Fort Washington, former clerk of courts at Hamilton County, and an ex-congressman, died thirty days after taking office.

WHEN CHARLES DICKENS visited Cincinnati, he was entertained at the Edmund Dexter residence (shown here some years after the visit). Dickens found the area at the northeast corner of Fourth and Broadway "cheerful, thriving, and animated." The Western-Southern Life Insurance Company is on this site today.

[19]

LOWER BROADWAY, south of Fourth Street, was the most fashionable residential area of the city in 1841.

CINCINNATI in 1845

SPIRES STRETCHED SKYWARD in Cincinnati as seen from Newport in 1852.

PIKE OPERA HOUSE opened on March 15, 1859, with the opera *Martha*. It was, for a time, Cincinnati's most sumptuous theatre until fire destroyed it in 1866.

ABRAHAM LINCOLN SPOKE on September 17, 1859, from a store balcony on the north side of Fifth Street, where the post office building is now.

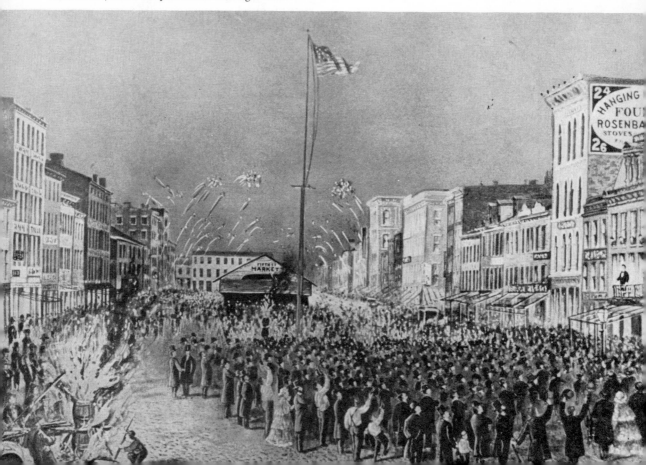

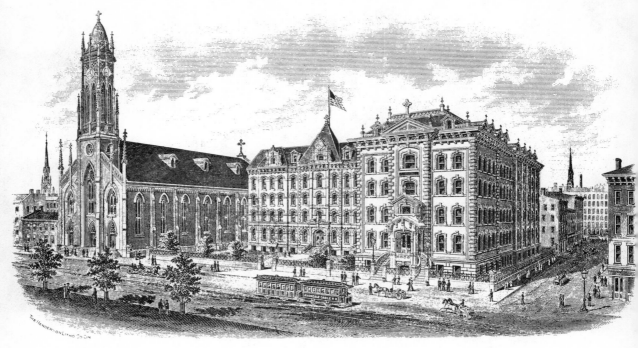

SAINT XAVIER CHURCH at 625 Sycamore Street was built on the site of the first Saint-Peter-In-Chains. Jesuits were given responsibility for the parish when the cathedral moved in 1845. The present church was completed in 1860 and later gutted by fire. The buildings beside it belong to Saint Xavier College, and later to the High School. In October of 1831, the college was established by Bishop Fenwick under the name Athenaeum. In 1840, it too was transferred to the Society of Jesus by Archbishop Purcell.

THE FIRST OHIO CAVALRY REGIMENT of the Civil War boards a steamboat, heading for action in 1861.

War and Peace: 1860 to 1870

THREE SIGNIFICANT THINGS happened to Cincinnati starting in the decade of 1860. First, the Civil War began, and many local men marched to what they were sure would be an easy victory for the North. Instead, the war dragged on. Cincinnati's manufacturers contributed greatly to the war effort and greatly increased their personal wealth. Uniforms and saddlery, shoes and the ever-present pork flowed to Union troops. Guns were rifled, steamboats iron clad. On Mount Adams, eight cannon zeroed their sights across the river, waiting for an enemy who never came.

There was a distinct threat once when twelve thousand Confederate troops led by Edmund Kirby Smith marched toward Cincinnati in an attempted invasion of the North. September 2, 1862, saw Cincinnati under martial law imposed by Union General Lew Wallace (who later wrote *Ben Hur*). A hasty pontoon bridge was thrown across the river. Within five days, seventy thousand men had crossed the river and were in place on the hills behind Covington. The Southern army turned back, and the Siege of Cincinnati was over. Nearly a year later, on July 13, 1863, John Morgan's Confederate raiders passed north and east of the city, and martial law was again declared. The fast-striking, hard-riding Morgan men vanished as quickly and as innocently as they had appeared.

The quick crossing of the Ohio by Wallace's men provided the impetus for one of the most important events in all Cincinnati's history—the building of the Suspension Bridge.

The foundations for the Suspension Bridge were set at the start of the war, but no cable had been strung. The bridge had faced such seemingly impossible problems that one historian called it "the bridge that couldn't be built."

First, there were bridge failures across the Licking River, and at Wheeling, West Virginia, public confidence faded and bond subscriptions dwindled. Legislators in

[23]

WILLIAM HAINES LYTLE was a unique blend: he was a poet, a lawyer, and a Brigadier General who died a hero's death at the battle of Chickamauga during the Civil War. The Lytle family owned much of the property in the area around the Taft Museum, one of the elite residential sections in Cincinnati's early history.

Ohio and Kentucky made such irrational demands that the bridge could not be lined up with Vine Street in Cincinnati or Scott Street in Covington. Ohio legislators wanted the span to be 1,400 feet long and 122 feet above the low-water level. The New York office of the Ohio Life Insurance Company went bankrupt in the Panic of 1857, and a run on the banks dried up financing.

But the need for the bridge had been proved by the urgency of getting people across the river during the Siege. By September 1865 the bridge towers were completed. They were 230 feet tall and 1,057 feet apart. On October 4, at 11 a.m., two cables and a footbridge were completed. The job of stringing the cables, 5,180 one-eighth-inch wires for each, ended on June 23, 1866. Each cable was 12-1/2 inches in diameter and weighed a million pounds. On the second day the bridge was open (December 2, 1866), 120,000 people walked across the Ohio River.

The bridge was engineered, built, and supervised by John A. Roebling and his son Washington. Roebling went on to build the Brooklyn Bridge, but his bridge across the Ohio was a classic and an important link in Cincinnati's history. During the 1937 flood of Cincinnati, it was the only bridge open across the Ohio from Cairo, Illinois to Steubenville, Ohio—some six hundred miles.

Significant in the decade was a slow realization that something was seriously wrong with Cincinnati's postwar commercial life. People passed by cramped, crowded Cincinnati as they headed West. Goods were not moving as they had before. Southern markets Cincinnati thought it had "owned" were trading with upstarts like Chicago, St. Louis, and Louisville. All three cities had better railroad

INDUSTRIAL CINCINNATI flexed its muscle to the utmost to outfit Union forces. Ironclad gunboats were built along the river's front.

NEARLY SEVENTY THOUSAND MEN marched across this pontoon bridge to head off an anticipated Confederate attack in 1862. The pontoons were in place near the site of the present Suspension Bridge. Cincinnati and its Kentucky neighbors were under martial law during the threat.

connections than Cincinnati. Prohibitive freight rates punished Cincinnati merchandise. Some Cincinnatians found their products shunted aside in Louisville as local merchandise there took priority.

Something needed to be done, and the city built itself a railroad. On Election Day, 1869, the voters taxed themselves into the railroad business. (Cincinnati still owns what now is a link in Southern Railway trackage—from here to Chattanooga.) Perhaps the voters were agreeable because the Cincinnati Redstockings had gone undefeated as the first-ever professional baseball team.

[26]

LEVI COFFIN was the president of the underground railroad which is reported to have helped more than three thousand blacks escape from slavery to freedom. He maintained an office at the northwest corner of Sixth and Elm, and it is said tunnels leading from the river to his office helped the slaves escape. From the Sixth and Elm site other tunnels spread to other buildings in the city as the blacks headed north to freedom. Coffin's home, pictured here, was at 3131 Wehrman and was close to the Beecher homestead. Coffin supposedly had a significant influence on Harriet Beecher Stowe in her writing the book *Uncle Tom's Cabin*.

MANY THOUGHT of Cincinnati as the political capital of the country for almost thirty years. Cincinnatian Salmon P. Chase, governor, U. S. Senator, and Chief Justice of the United States, was a founder of the Republican Party. Chase was joined on the Supreme Court by John McLean. Senator George H. Pendleton served in the Congress at that time. Lincoln called on three from Cincinnati to serve in his cabinet: Chase, as Secretary of the Treasury, Edwin Stanton, who practiced law here, as Secretary of War; and Cincinnati native William Dennison as Postmaster General.

WHEN THE BURNET HOUSE opened in 1850, it was called the finest hotel in the world by the *Illustrated London News.* Here, in 1864, Gen. U. S. Grant and Gen. William Tecumseh Sherman planned the March through Georgia. Burnet House was built on property owned by Judge Jacob Burnet, behind the site of the Union Trust Tower.

BARREN-LOOKING MOUNT ADAMS, seen in the background, was controlled by Nicholas Long-worth and his family, when he died in 1863 in his eighty-first year. He had at one time grown grapes all along the hill, until black rot ruined the vines. Longworth at one time owned the Baum home at Third and Pike streets, and paid more property taxes in the mid-nineteenth century than anyone in America except New York's William Astor.

SPIRES SYMBOLIC of religious brotherhood dominated the Cincinnati skyline in 1866. The single spire of Saint Peter-In-Chains rose 221 feet above the church built in 1845. It was the cathedral of the Cincinnati Catholic Archdiocese. When this picture was taken, work had just been completed on the twin towers of the Plum Street Temple across from the cathedral. Dr. Isaac Mayer Wise, one of American Jewry's great figures, planned the synagogue.

SUSPENSION BRIDGE, built in the 1860s, was soon to have an economic impact on the ferryboats that plied the river at the end of the decade.

STEAMBOATS LINED UP at the Public Landing after the Civil War, as trade was resumed with the South. This was the scene in 1865.

DOCK HANDS worked to unload the steamboats in Cincinnati in the 1860s. It was toward the end of this decade that Lafcadio Hearn began writing in Cincinnati, and tales of his later visits to the levee and to the black community of Cincinnati were among his more popular writings.

THE FIRST PROFESSIONAL BASEBALL team in 1869 sported the Big C of Cincinnati. From left: Calvin McVey, Charles Gould, Harry Wright, George Wright, Fred Waterman, Andy Leonard, Doug Allison, Asa Brainard, and Charles Sweasy.

Extra Niceties: 1870 to 1880

THE FLOWER OF CINCINNATI bloomed as never before. If commercial problems were on the minds of many, the city was glowing with artistic good health and *gemütlichkeit*. The Public Library moved into the half-finished Handy Opera House, now gone from Vine Street. The Cincinnati Society of Natural History was organized in 1870. The Historical and Philosophical Society of Ohio moved onto Walnut between Fourth and Fifth Streets and got a new lease on life. A series of free concerts in Burnet Woods was endowed by William S. Groesbeck, and free concerts are still presented in the parks.

The census showed a population of 216,239 for the decade 1870-1880. City Council was reorganized and a board of aldermen established. Way out in Avondale, in September 1875, Andrew Erkenbrecher opened his Zoological Gardens. Eden Park and Burnet Woods were developed. The citizens voted $100,000 for park bonds. Annexation added seventeen square miles to Cincinnati, up from seven in 1868. The Panic of 1873 rocked the city's financial community, and cholera killed three thousand people; but the Grand Opera House and the Grand Hotel—both gone now—were built and opened. D. J. Kenny published *Illustrated Cincinnati*. The National Republican Convention was held here in 1876 and nominated Rutherford B. Hayes, once Cincinnati's city solicitor. The Chamber of Commerce Building, which later burned, and the Government Building were built.

But four events outdid all others: "The Fountain" was dedicated, the first incline clambered up the hills of Mount Auburn, Music Hall was built, and industrial expositions caught the eye of America.

The Tyler Davidson Memorial Fountain is Cincinnati. It has serenely held court as the focal point of downtown Cincinnati since October 6, 1871, when it was dedicated on the spot where the Fifth Street Market had been. The Fountain was the gift of leading merchant Henry Probasco, who offered it to the city in honor of his brother-in-law, Davidson, and purchased it in Bavaria where it had been cast from old bronze cannon.

Population growth in the 1870s was slow compared with the giddy increases earlier in the century. Cincinnati was cramped for space, for room to grow. The debut in 1872 of the incline up Mount Auburn proved that the many hillsides around the city were habitable year-round. Cincinnati could stretch out. There was city-wide growpower again.

Five "inclined-plane railways" were built in Cincinnati between 1875 and 1890. The Price Hill Incline was opened in 1875 and was used until 1943. In 1876 the Clifton Incline ran up McMicken Avenue to what is now Bellevue Hill Park. It was abandoned in 1926. Perhaps the most famous and certainly the most popular was the Mount Adams Incline, which opened in 1876 and carried pedestrians and streetcars up and down the hill until April 1948, when it was shut down for repair. In 1952 the plane and the machinery were dismantled. In 1954 the power plant was demolished, despite an appeal for subscriptions to save it. The ticket office fell in the path of Interstate access roads in the 1970s.

The last incline was Fairview, which opened in 1894 to carry Crosstown streetcars from McMillan to McMicken streets. It closed in 1924.

At the top of each incline except Fairview, lavish establishments called hilltop houses were built. People swarmed the inclines to get above the city's smoky air to enjoy the view, the food, and the entertainment. The Highland House at the top of Mount Adams became known as the best hilltop house in town, with room for eight thousand patrons. Often people in the crowded basin gawked up at the fireworks displays of summer.

From the top of each incline private streetcar and railroad lines branched out, assuring expansion of the city.

Industrial expositions were not unique to Cincinnati, but Cincinnati regarded them uniquely. The first exposition, in 1869, was dimmed by the ones that followed. (America's 1876 Centennial Exposition was held in Philadelphia.)

Merchants knew that the exposition was an unbeatable showcase for their wares. Each year more and more people came to see the equipment on display, and Cincinnatians loved to show what they had. The Fountain was dedicated at the conclusion of the Exposition of 1871. The parade that opened the 1875 exposition was five miles long. By the end of the decade, exhibitors from all across the country crowded the town.

The expositions ended after the largest one of all, the Cincinnati Centennial Exposition of 1888. Machinery Hall, three blocks long, was built over the Miami Canal. Gondolas were imported from Venice. Steam and electricity were the hits of the show, and some manufacturers set up small plants to produce items during the one-hundred-day exposition. No one could top the Exposition of 1888, and no more like that were ever held.

Reuben Springer, one of the city's benefactors, listened to the May Festival in 1875 as rain pelted the tin roof of Saengerhall, distracting the passionate audience.

CITY WORKERS moved in on Friday, February 4, 1870, to demolish the Fifth Street Market, because something had to come down to make room for Fountain Square. Since then, the mayor of Cincinnati has made a purchase on the square once a year to satisfy a tradition that the area be used as a market place.

THE ROYAL FOUNDRY of Bavaria in Munich tested the fountain before it was disassembled and shipped to Cincinnati in the spring of 1871. Henry Probasco had found the fountain at the foundry on a European trip in his quest "for a permanent object of beauty and utility" as a gift to his city and a monument to his brother-in-law and partner, Tyler Davidson.

Springer pledged $150,000 to build an appropriate music hall if public donations would match the amount. The public contributed but the funds were still short of the estimates, and Springer put up $125,000 more. The building, a gem of acoustical excellence, opened in 1878. Music Hall was recently renovated through the beneficence of philanthropists Ralph and Patricia Corbett.

THE TYLER-DAVIDSON MEMORIAL FOUNTAIN was first viewed by the public on October 6, 1871, following a procession of celebrities which started from the Burnet House. Rutherford B. Hayes, governor of Ohio and later president, was one of the key speakers at the dedication. More than twenty thousand people attended as the light fabric slipped off the Genius of Waters, unveiling it to public view.

ORMSBY MacKNIGHT MITCHEL wanted to build an observatory in Cincinnati that would rival one recently completed in Russia. Mitchel was "determined to show the autocrat of all the Russias that an obscure individual in this wilderness city in a republican country can raise more money here by voluntary gift in behalf of science than his majesty can raise. . . ." Money was raised, and the observatory was built on the Longworth property on Mount Ida. The hill was renamed Mount Adams after John Quincy Adams had given the dedication speech in 1843 at Wesley Chapel. The observatory became part of the University of Cincinnati in 1872 and was moved to land donated by John Kilgour on Mount Lookout.

THE UNITED STATES POST OFFICE stood at the southwest corner of Fourth and Vine streets until 1886. It was replaced by the Chamber of Commerce Building, and now the Central Trust Tower is on the site.

WILLIAM HOLMES McGUFFEY is the author of a series of books read by an estimated one hundred million people. *McGuffey's Eclectic Readers* were the educational backbone of the American system from 1836 to the early 1900s. The books were famed for their homilies, proverbs, and patriotic expressions.

THE GIBSON HOUSE was enlarged to handle three hundred guests in 1873. The room rate was $4.

WORK WAS STARTED in 1874 on the Government Building on the north side of Fifth Street between Main and Walnut. It took thirteen years to complete, and was described as French Renaissance in style.

THE HEAVY PALL OF SMOKE that Cincinnati's manufacturing might created shows clearly in this lithograph of 1875. Between factories and steamboats, the sky was often thick and gray.

DR. ISAAC M. WISE was one of the most influential Jews in America. He was founder and president of Hebrew Union College in 1875, and started Reform Judaism in America. It was his feeling that Judaism in America should have an American scope and inspiration. He died in 1900. His granddaughter, Iphegene Bettman, was a columnist for the *Times-Star* and mother of Common Pleas Judge Gilbert Bettman.

HENRY HUSCHARD MEYER founded in 1876 the meat company which evolved into the H. H. Meyer Packing Company. The company was one of the first to identify its pork products with a brand name. Since meat quality at that time, particularly pork, was difficult to control, many butchers sought anonymity. The photo at left shows the Partridge butchers at a retail outlet.

BUSINESSES START in interesting ways. It's been said that Joseph Thomas Carew and Christopher R. Mabley were passing through Cincinnati on a business trip to Memphis in 1877. Having missed their connection here, they walked around town and reached Fountain Square, saw a "For Rent" sign, and decided that 66 Fifth Street was a fine place for a store. Carew was the first in Cincinnati to adopt full-page newspaper ads, to give elaborate Christmas performances, and to set up the Arbor Day custom. The old Mabley and Carew Building was once illuminated by 10,000 lights that glimmered opposite Fountain Square.

CLOVERNOOK HOME FOR THE BLIND began at the Cary Cottage, shown here in a wood carving. Two sisters, Alice and Phoebe Cary, were born on the 27-acre farm their father had built at 6990 Hamilton Avenue in North College Hill. The women were accomplished poets and famed in America and England for the simplicity and originality of their works, the British calling them pure products of American life.

THE MOUNT ADAMS INCLINE and the Highland House beside it under construction, are shown in this mid 1870s view from East Fifth Street. From the Mount Adams Incline *(below),* completed in 1875, Cincinnati looked like this. Through the haze and smoke the Suspension Bridge can be seen in the background.

[39]

THE STEAM ENGINE and the passenger car were all one on the Mount Lookout Dummy line that served Delta and Erie avenues to the Eastern Avenue car barns. The line ran from about 1863 to 1897. Its final route, after two extensions, was from Delta and Erie to Eastern Avenue near the East End Car Barn, with a branch out Eastern to Columbia.

THE PRICE HILL INCLINE, a continuation of West Eighth Street up Price Hill, was one year old in 1875. It rose 350 feet high with a double track 800 feet long. The incline was built by William Price with funds supplied by his father, Gen. Reese Price. The horsecar on the left was from the Riverside and Sedamville Line. Unlike most of the inclines of the era, alcohol was not served at the top, giving the hill the name Buttermilk Mountain. A number of saloons, including First Choice, Next Chance, and Last Chance, reminded travelers that they were about to scale the heights to abstemious Buttermilk Mountain.

THE SEVENTH Industrial Exposition of September 10 to October 10, 1879, in the Music Hall of the Grand Permanent Building, was crammed with merchandise and visitors, marking the growth of the city in the ninety-odd years since its founding.

THE GAMBRINUS STOCK COMPANY built this huge barrel to advertise its barrel-making prowess at the Cincinnati Industrial Exposition of 1879. The capacity of the barrel was said to be 16,500 gallons and, it is assumed, was empty when the horses pulled it along the parade route.

WHEN CINCINNATI'S PUBLIC landing was the center of commerce, all available space was used for storage and preparation for shipment. Barrels of salt pork or booze stood in casually stacked allotments waiting for steamboats to dock and take the freight on board.

STEAMBOATS played such a large part in Cincinnati's development because of the mass of material they could move. A steamboat, loaded down with what appears to be cotton bales, docked near Cincinnati. The steamboat's wide beam and shallow draught made it possible to move cargo on the river in almost all seasons.

A RAINY DAY on a steamboat eliminated the opportunity to prowl about the decks. Here passengers gathered about the pot-bellied stove to keep warm as the steamboat left Cincinnati. It appears as if the photographer sat with his back to the camera and ran a cord to snap the picture once he felt he was properly positioned.

A Birthday Celebrated, An Era Ended: 1880 to 1890

THE CENSUS OF 1880 showed that forty thousand more people lived here than a decade previously. The suburbs tentacled out over the hilltops. The first train on the Cincinnati Southern Railroad went through to Chattanooga, and southern markets were more accessible again. Opening of the track was celebrated with a banquet for three thousand at Music Hall. The Democrats convened here in 1880 and nominated Winfield Scott Hancock to oppose James A. Garfield. The *Times* and the *Star* merged under the guidance of Charles P. Taft, and E. W. Scripps was putting out his *Penny Paper,* later the *Post*. The *Enquirer,* founded in 1841, had just lost Lafcadio Hearne to the *Commercial.* A company was formed to light the city with electricity. There were problems with Sunday closing laws.

It was the decade in which the river's importance began to diminish. Straight, slender rail replaced the winding waterways. La Belle Riviere—which had made Cincinnati what it was—gave way to the steam locomotive. In 1884 the river responded to this slight with the worst flood yet in Cincinnati's history. The city waterworks pumping stations stopped. The gasworks were flooded, and the city went dark. Some fifteen hundred business houses were flooded; twenty-four hundred people were homeless. On Valentine's Day the river stood at 71-3/4 feet. Railroad traffic was cut off. Access to homes on Third Street was by rowboat into the second-story windows. But the waters abated, as they always do.

The next year Cincinnati paid the price of lawlessness. Two young men were accused of killing their employer, and the state had an airtight case. But the county jail was already crammed with convicted murderers serving light sentences, and William Berner, one of the defendants, was found guilty only of manslaughter. Although Judge Stanley Matthews denounced the jurymen and gave Berner the maximum sentence of twenty years, a sense of outrage flowed through the town. That night,

THE FLOOD OF 1884 brought the water higher than ever before in Cincinnati. Workers here on Pearl Street, between Walnut and Vine streets, paused in their boats to look at the cameraman. Hats, especially the derby, were derigueur.

[44]

THE COURTHOUSE RIOT of March 28 and 29, 1884, started at a "public indignation meeting" at Music Hall when an unidentified man incited a mob to converge on the jail to lynch William Berner, accused of murdering his employer, William Kirk, with the help of another youth, Joe Palmer. Federal troops erected barricades on Court Street, looking toward the jail.

THERE HAD INDEED BEEN some justification for the outburst of fury on the part of the citizenry because of political misrule and the rather loose, questionable conduct of city and county affairs. But it hardly could justify the more than fifty dead and 300 wounded, and the destruction of the Hamilton County Courthouse, whose Law Library *(above)* is a mute witness to the disaster. A Gatling gun, seen in the center of the picture *(below)*, was credited with restoring sense and sensibility to the city.

March 28, 1884, there was an indignant meeting at Music Hall. Leading citizens spoke on laxness in the administration of justice. The tone of the meeting was temperate. The outcome was not.

A young man leaving Music Hall shouted, "To the jail!" and the Courthouse Riot had begun. Three days later fifty-four people had died and more than three hundred had been injured; the Courthouse had burned to the ground, destroying most of Hamilton County's records.

In 1886, thirty-two years after the idea had been proposed, the Cincinnati Art Museum and the affiliated art school became realities. A dynamic group of women had started the museum drive in 1877. Their enthusiasm was such that Charles W. West pledged $150,000 for the museum if the public would match the amount. The match was made and West provided still another $150,000. City Council, over the objections of the park commissioner, allowed the erection of buildings atop Eden Park. In 1884 Rookwood Pottery also was established on Mount Adams, having moved from its first home on Eastern Avenue on the bank of the river.

Also between 1880 and 1890: the first cable car ran up Gilbert Avenue at the rate of eight miles an hour. A man named Hudepohl bought a brewery, and John L. Sullivan was signed to fight in Chester Park on Spring Grove Avenue. The state legislature ruled that blacks should be taught in the public schools. The first telephone exchange went into operation in 1887. Procter and Gamble, makers of that floating soap, moved to the new Ivorydale plant along Mill Creek following the fire on Central Avenue. A million people came to Cincinnati's birthday party in 1888.

But as the decade closed there were only five thousand steamboat departures or arrivals. Scarcely more than a quarter-million hogs were butchered. An era had ended.

THE SIXTH STREET MARKET between Plum and Central was another Cincinnati tradition until it was torn down for access to an expressway. A congregation of produce men paused for the cameraman around the 1880s. At its height, there were 111 stands outside and 64 stands inside the building. The Jabez Elliott flower market stood one block away, between Elm and Plum.

JAMES PARKER found his apple orchard more valuable as a picnic spot than an apple-producing farm in the early 1880s. He built several buildings, including a dance hall, the forerunner to Moonlite Gardens at old Coney Island.

THE FORESTRY CONGRESS at Cincinnati began the national tradition of Arbor Day in 1882. Cincinnati's Superintendent of Schools, John B. Peaslee, took up the idea with a public school-oriented pageant that planted the Presidential Groves in Eden Park. Later, the Mabley and Carew Company initiated a program to give a flowering shrub to each school child up to the sixth grade as an annual commemoration. Mabley and Carew donated in this manner more than 5.2 million trees to Cincinnati youngsters during a fifty-year period.

[47]

SPRING GROVE is Cincinnati's cemetery. "Only a place with a heart and soul could make for their dead a more magnificent park than any which exists for their living," said artist Emma Calve about Spring Grove. The cemetery, founded after efforts of Daniel Drake, is 782 acres large and an exceptional arboretum. Many Civil War generals are buried here. Shown is the tomb of Charles W. West, founder of the Art Museum.

JOSEPH EARNSHAW surveyed in January of 1886 the rather narrow, 44-feet-two-and-a-quarter inches of the first H. & S. Pogue store on Fourth Street *(left)*. The site was almost two hundred feet deep and butted the Emery Building behind it. The Irish brothers, Henry and Samuel Pogue, headed the large prosperous store. The soft goods department of later years *(below)* featured just one fan. The overhead track carried orders and cash to a clerk for proper change. This eliminated the need for cash registers but often created delays for the customers.

THE CART coming up the road was on the big bend on Erie Avenue which was called the Horseshoe Bend of Hyde Park Canyon. The roadway was built at a cost of more than $40,000 so a streetcar line could stretch out to Madisonville. Where the bend juts out now stands a Cincinnati Police District headquarters. St. John's Park, as it was known, is in the right foreground.

HAUCK'S BREWERS gathered in front of the brewery to promote Hauck's lager beer, one of Cincinnati's best. The Miami Purchase Association has restored the Hauck home on historic Dayton Street.

WHEN CINCINNATI CELEBRATED its 100th birthday in 1888, the Centennial Exposition *(above)* was the biggest and the best ever put on in Cincinnati. The north quarter of the Main Exposition Hall held displays and merchandise from some of Cincinnati's leading merchants and manufacturers. Other celebrations included this Grand Procession of the Order of **Cincinnati** *(left)*, saved for posterity in a drawing by Henry Farny.

TWIN TOWERS mark the entrance to the three-block-long building over the Miami-Erie Canal. It was specially built for the 1888 celebration that ran from July 4 to November 10. More than a million persons attended what was formally billed as the Centennial Exposition of the Ohio Valley and Central States. Described as a "double-barreled, rolicking fair," its visitors even had imported gondolas *(below)* at their disposal.

THE WOODEN INDIAN on Front and Broadway at the entrance of the Spencer House, which had been one of the city's fine early hotels, experienced a smoky view of the river and the Suspension Bridge in 1889.

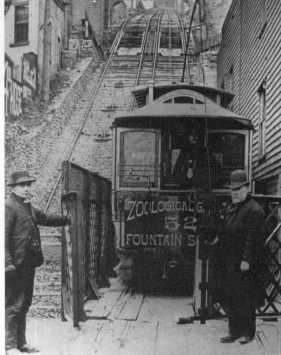

THE MOUNT AUBURN INCLINE, built in 1872, was also known as the Main Street, Lookout Incline, and Mount Auburn Line. In 1884 it was helpful in getting visitors to the zoo, which had opened nine years earlier. The inclines promoted growth of the city's hilltops.

[52]

TRANSPORTATION at the top of the inclines was supplied by horse and mule cars which traveled the main roads. Cars would connect visitors with the suburban shuttles. This scene in late 1889 is at Reading Road and Oak Street.

Political Problems and Mechanical Might: 1890 to 1900

CINCINNATI BUILT half of America's carriages and carts between 1890 and 1900, when Henry Ford was tinkering with automobiles in Detroit. The country was in the Gay Nineties but Cincinnati had a severe case of the political doldrums.

Republican George B. Cox first ran for office when Democratic policemen pestered him and the patrons of his saloon. Cox decided that a dab of political power would stop the harassment, and he successfully ran for City Council. The year was 1877. By 1886 Cox had the town locked up. The governor, Joseph B. Foraker, abolished the elected Board of Public Works and made it the appointed Board of Public Affairs, thus releasing two thousand patronage jobs. Chairman of that Board — George B. Cox.

People outside the city began calling Cincinnati "corrupt and contented, the worst-governed city in the United States." And Cox ran it smugly from the Mecca Bar on Walnut and Wielert's, in the Over-the-Rhine area.

But there was work to be done as the turn of the century approached. Cincinnati at that time had the largest soap factory in the country, as well as the largest playing card factory, trunk factory, tannery, compressed yeast factory, tube and pipe works, printing ink plant, harness and saddlery works, theatrical publishing house, ladies' shoe factory, and office furniture factory. By 1898 Cincinnati encompassed 35-1/4 square miles. Westwood, Clifton, and Avondale had joined the city. The Central Bridge opened to Newport, the Business Men's Club (Cincinnati Club) was formed. The brand new City Hall was dedicated, and the first concrete bridge in the United States was built in Eden Park. The Cincinnati Symphony Orchestra was formed under the baton of Frank Van der Stucken. At the University of Cincinnati McMicken Hall, the first building on the present U.C. campus, was dedicated. And that faint rumble on October 31, 1895, really was an earthquake.

A TOLLGATE guarded the Carthage Pike—Spring Grove Avenue intersection in Carthage in 1890. Robert Morris (right) was gatekeeper for the last 17 years until the gates were done away with in 1900. Spring Grove Avenue runs to the right of the picture. Carthage Pike is the roadway in front.

MAYBE NOT THE EASIEST WAY to get to Hamilton in 1890 was a stagecoach, but one still ran from Sixth and Main.

THE RIVER was full of small boats when scale models of the *Niña, Pinta,* and *Santa Maria* sailed the Ohio to celebrate America's discovery 400 years earlier.

TIMES CHANGE, and certainly the faculty at Hughes High School has changed since this picture was taken in 1891. The school, named after Thomas Hughes, an English cobbler, was built partly as a result of a bequest he left after his death in 1824. The first Hughes school was built at Fifth and Mound. The present Hughes High School was built in 1910.

THE FINAL SPAN of the Central Bridge *(above)* went into place in 1893. It was the last bridge to be built in Cincinnati until the Brent Spence Bridge. The opening celebrations *(below)* were a festive affair, with flags fluttering in the breeze, seen here at the foot of Broadway.

CITY HALL at Ninth and Plum *(right)* was nearing completion in the early 1890s. Saint-Peter-In-Chains and Wise Temple stand on two of the other Ninth and Plum corners, making the intersection "inspiring," as one punster said. An idea of the internal opulence of City Hall can be had by glancing at the mayor's outer office *(below)* on dedication day.

THE DEDICATION of the new City Hall on May 13, 1893 was a festive event even though the city was firmly in the hands of political boss George Cox. "The building is justly conceded to be the most elegant structure of its kind in the United States," a historian noted. The building, handsome as ever externally, is now cramped, crowded, and obsolescent.

BESIDES BEING the spot from which George Cox ran Cincinnati, Wielert's cafe was typical of the Vine Street hot spots. In the late 1890s, there were 113 places between McMillan and Vine streets where thirsty Cincinnatians could wet their whistles. There were 23 in one block between Twelfth and Thirteenth Streets alone. Wielert's Garden was in the next block at 1408 Vine Street.

FIFTH AND WALNUT has always been a busy Cincinnati intersection. In 1893 the streets looked like a track layer's delight. The present entrance to Fountain Square would eventually be built in the upper left corner of the picture. The block would go through two other demolish-build cycles before DuBois Tower would stand there.

IT WAS AN IMPRESSIVE MOMENT for the twenty-two assembled dignitaries as the first long distance call to New York was made in December of 1893. The man on the phone was Mayor John B. Mosby.

ANNA AND ANDREW JERGENS posed beside their 1615 Bruce Avenue home. He began his lotion and soap empire in 1882 and moved it to the Spring Grove Avenue plants in 1894.

CINCINNATI has had a long and rich banking tradition. Before the mergers and consolidations which gave the city the five major banks it has today, there were many separate and independent banks around the city. In 1893, this was the banking scene in the Fifth National Bank tellers' area. The bank was on the first floor of the Chamber of Commerce Building.

THE COLUMBIA THEATER "for 10 years was one of the leading vaudeville theaters in the world," a publicist happily proclaimed. The theater originally opened onto an alley on Carew Place about where the entrance to Fountain Square from Sixth is today. The Columbia later became the Keith's Theater and opened onto Walnut Street.

IN OAKLEY, a magnificent pony emporium was in operation during the 1890s. Crooked races and a state law against betting forced the closing of the track. The track was converted to homesites for the workers at Cincinnati Milling Machine which moved out there in 1907.

NO ONE KNOWS whether this photograph was from a fashion show—but tennis has always been popular in Cincinnati. Stewart Shillito laid out the city's first court in 1878, and there were six active tennis clubs by 1889.

LITTLE IS KNOWN about the Brighton Bicycle Club except that the members celebrated with elan and enthusiam when they reached their destinations on their bicycles. They appear to have been some of the city's genuine "big wheels."

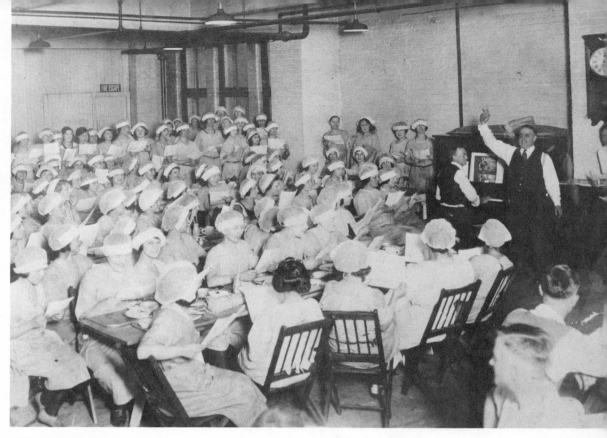

CRACKER WRAPPERS and packagers at the Streitman Biscuit Company seem to be led in song during lunch. Photographic notes do not indicate if this was a special celebration or a daily event at the bakery.

CREATION OF A CIGAR required intricate handwork. Workers at the Ibold Cigar Company were skilled practitioners of the cigar-rolling craft.

THE UNIVERSITY OF CINCINNATI moved to Burnet Woods and its Clifton location in the 1890s. McMicken Hall *(left)* was built as a result of Charles McMicken's $1 million gift. That was followed by Hanna and Cunningham halls and the Van Wormer Library. U.C. history is spiced with firsts and innovations. William H. McGuffey, while president of Cincinnati College, published the first four of his *Eclectic Readers* here. It was one of the earliest western colleges to teach natural science. U.C. offered one of the first courses in civil engineering and established one of the first professorships of music. U.C. was the first municipal university in Ohio, and the birthplace of the co-operative system of technological education. Daniel Drake, father of western medicine, founded the Medical College in 1819 and revived Cincinnati College in 1835.

FRANK DUVENECK, here teaching a life painting class in the 1890s, was almost solely responsible for the city's reputation as a major art center around the turn of the century. Duveneck was born in Covington in 1848 and studied in Europe, where he earned fame as a painter and as a teacher. He returned to Cincinnati in 1888 to join the staff of the Cincinnati Art Academy. Artists flocked to Cincinnati to study with Duveneck, and a gallery at the Art Museum is devoted to his works. Duveneck was president of the Cincinnati Art Club and Dean of the Art Academy until his death in 1919.

A Decade of Calm: 1900 to 1910

THE TOWN still belonged to Cox and his henchmen, Rudolph Hynicka and August Herrmann, but interesting events were afoot. In Washington, D.C., Alice Roosevelt married Congressman Nicholas Longworth of Cincinnati. White House weddings spawn national interest, and this one had Cincinnati agog in 1906.

In the same year down at the northeast corner of Fourth and Vine, a peculiar thing was going on. The first poured concrete building was being constructed. An awed but cynical city editor of the morning *Cincinnati Enquirer* spent the first night of the completed building's life waiting for its collapse and an eyewitness story.

Hyde Park, Evanston, Bond Hill, and Winton Place were annexed to Cincinnati along with Silverton, Roselawn, and South Cumminsville. In 1905 speed limits were passed. You could go seven miles an hour in downtown and fifteen miles an hour in the suburbs. The symphony season was called off in 1907 because of union trouble, but two years later Leopold Stokowski was named conductor.

At Third and Pike, William Howard Taft accepted the Republican party's nomination for the presidency on the front porch of Charles P. Taft's house. That was 1908. The next year, Cincinnati Milling Machine moved all the way out to Oakley, and American Laundry Machine Company started up in Norwood.

In Covington, Dan Beard's Sons of Daniel Boone merged with Sir Robert Baden-Powell's Boy Scouts of England, and the Boy Scouts were born in America in 1908. The Grand Opera House burned down a couple of years before the second Pike Opera House fire. A system of parks was designed for the city.

ASA VAN WORMER, who had less than one year of schooling, donated the building on the right to the University of Cincinnati in 1900 as the college's library, today's administration building. Off to the left are Hanna Hall, McMicken Hall, and Cunningham Hall which housed McMicken College of Liberal Arts.

HENRY FARNY (left), the artist who sketched much of the city's early history for *Harper's Weekly,* chatted with Theodore Roosevelt when Roosevelt visited the Cincinnati Zoo. Roosevelt felt the nation owed Farny a special debt for detailing the life of America's Indians. Farny, ranking just behind Duveneck in Cincinnati's artistic hierarchy, also did 76 illustrations for McGuffey's *Eclectic Readers,* starting in 1879. Farny had studios on Third Street, Fourth Street, and his last was on Straight Street. He died in 1916 at the age of 69.

THE *Island Queen* tied up at the converted Parker's Grove at the turn of the century: One of the early officials of the "Coney Island of the West" was Thomas W. Paxton who stated this company policy: "We intend that everything shall be first class. All ladies and children will be as safe here as at home. We are determined to protect them, and all bad characters will be made to keep straight or be excluded. The boats will run regularly even if there isn't a passenger." The *Island Queen* itself had five decks, a capacity of 4,000 passengers, a ballroom floor of 20,000 square feet, and 7,000 lights.

CINCINNATI'S FINEST stood for inspection inside the Police Gymnasium at the turn of the century. In 1803, a year after Cincinnati was incorporated as a village, a night watch of volunteers was established. In 1834, police were paid, and in 1842, two men were to work as policemen in the daytime. In 1886, a non-partisan police department (earlier police were members of the party in power and had some impact on the voters) was established. After that reorganization, only twelve members of the original force remained on duty, and a whole new Police Division came into operation. Cincinnati has long been regarded as having a good police force.

VOLUNTEER FIREMEN have played an important role in the history of Cincinnati and surrounding areas, such as the Oakley volunteer fire department (before Oakley became a part of Cincinnati), shown at right. But in Cincinnati proper, a paid department was established as early as in 1853, after an outrageous incident occurred where ten different volunteer companies arrived at a lumberyard fire and fought each other instead of putting out the fire. The paid department has ever since had a tradition of excellence in its training programs. Here the drills paid off, as firemen *(below)* responded to a turn-of-the-century alarm.

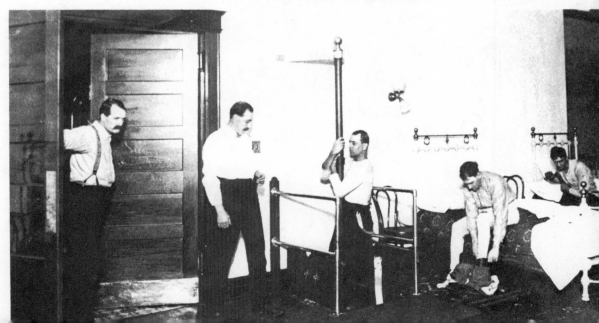

BY 1900, A TELEPHONE could be installed in one's home with the help of a dapper installer.

BEFORE THE AUTO BEGAN TO appear on Cincinnati's streets, there was nothing wrong with having a statue in the middle of an intersection. President Garfield stayed in the middle of Eighth at Race Street until vehicular traffic became such that he had to be moved to his present home in Piatt Park.

MOUNT HEALTHY got its name when Cincinnatians fled there from the dreaded cholera epidemics that often swept through the city. The first epidemic occurred in 1832. During the next sixty-eight years cholera returned seven times, and during the 1849 epidemic, the disease claimed 4,114 of Cincinnati's 116,000 population. Below is a pioneer picnic at Mount Healthy at the start of the century.

LAND SPECULATORS in 1901 could have snapped up a bargain at Colerain Pike looking north with Galbraith Road branching off to the west. The Wiesehahn Grocery and the Pioneer Inn are in the foreground. Groesbeck schoolhouse is on the left-hand side of the picture. This intersection is about a mile from the present Northgate Mall.

A NOVEL THING happened at Fourth and Vine streets in 1902. The Ingalls Building was the first reinforced concrete skyscraper in the world. The concrete was strengthened with steel rods, but one newspaperman knew it would not stand, and he waited all night for it to fall. And waited. And waited.

THE ORIGINAL GRAND OPERA HOUSE opened in September of 1874. After a January 1901 fire, the theater reopened a year later with *Ben Hur.* Later the theater was to become a movie house. It recently closed its doors. For many years it was the only theater in Cincinnati where one could smoke in the balcony.

[69]

THEY CALLED IT "The Palace of the Fans" back then in 1902. It was the grandstand, a double-decked one at that, and beer was a nickel. This was changed in 1912 when Redland Field opened complete with the right field bleachers. The grandstand was stretched out down both fields with just single decks. In 1927 the field boxes were added. The press box was added in 1938 and in 1939 a second deck of steel stands was erected over the single deck down both foul lines. Anxious fans could make Crosley Field throb when they stomped the steel decks in unison.

[70]

THE CINCINNATI RIDING CLUB in 1902 was located at Highland Avenue and Helen Street in Mount Auburn. Mount Auburn, one of the first suburbs of Cincinnati, prospered because of the spectacular view of the growing, crowded city beneath it. Comparatively easy access to downtown was responsible for its earliest development.

THESE SEVEN STALWARTS were the members of the University of Cincinnati's first basketball team in 1902.

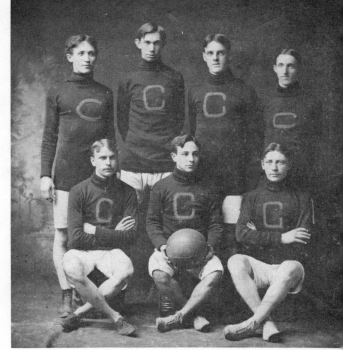

RUDOLPH HYNICKA, police clerk, chief clerk, Hamilton County treasurer, and chairman of the Hamilton County Republican party, was George Cox's patronage manager. He controlled a chain of forty burlesque and legitimate theater companies.

CARRIE NATION came to Cincinnati with hatchet in hand, ready to wage war against demon alcohol. Her first hatchet job was in Witchita in 1901. Later she came to Cincinnati, took one look at the bars along Vine Street and said, "I would have dropped from exhaustion before I went a block." At the Atlantic Garden, next to the Enquirer Building, a blond lush told the temperance leader she would mend her ways—and lifted Carrie's earrings at the same time.

THE CANAL in 1903 didn't have much traffic on it anymore. It was regarded as a cesspool and an eyesore.

PIKE'S OPERA HOUSE burned to the ground for the second time on February 26, 1903. This time the theater, which stood on Fourth Street between Vine and Walnut, would not be rebuilt.

THREE FAMED BUILDINGS stood side by side around 1903. At far left is the sign of the Palace Hotel, built in part by lantern light in 1882. The Atlantic Garden was a watering hole for Cincinnati's sports fans who watched John L. Sullivan earn $50 for boxing—with gloves on, an unappreciated nicety. The *Enquirer,* which was started on April 10, 1841, has published a Sunday edition longer than any paper in America. The newspaper moved to this location after the first Pike Opera House fire in 1866.

CHRIST CHURCH, the mother church of Cincinnati Episcopalians, has been anchored on Fourth Street since 1835. The church was organized in 1817 by Dr. Daniel Drake, William Henry Harrison, Arthur St. Clair, and Jacob Baymiller. It became a free church (with no charge for pews) in 1899.

ONE OF THE BEST EXAMPLES of early American architecture is the Baum House on Third and Pike streets. It was finished in 1820, right after Martin Baum *(above right)* had suffered reverses during the Panic of 1819. It is not clear whether he ever lived in the building. Baum was Cincinnati's first manufacturer, banker, and sugar refiner. He had interests in shipping, the literary society, the canal, and a large foundry. The building became, briefly, a female seminary until it was purchased by Nicholas Longworth in 1830. The home was sold again in 1866 to Francis Suire who, in turn, sold it to David Sinton, the hotelman. Sinton's daughter Anna married Charles P. Taft there in 1873 and it became the Taft home on Sinton's death in 1900.

THE NEWSROOM of the E. W. Scripps' *Cincinnati Post* looked up to date in 1907 with the most modern of copy desks. Alfred Segal, who was to write his column as Cincinnatus, is second from the left.

HERMAN SCHNEIDER quit school at the age of fourteen to work in the mine near his Pennsylvania home until he earned enough to continue his education. In 1906, at the age of thirty-four, Schneider was made Dean of the College of Engineering at the University of Cincinnati. Shortly after that he inaugurated his now-famous plan of cooperative engineering education. Under this plan, students spend alternating periods in the classroom studying theory and in shops or factories absorbing practical experience. Coordination of these two facets rounds out the student's education. Schneider later became President of the University of Cincinnati.

WHEN THE FIFTH Third Union Trust Company came into being in 1908, millions of dollars in securities and negotiable instruments were transported.

THE GIRLS from the Anna Louise Inn performed in the yard in front of the Union Bethel. The Union Bethel was one of Cincinnati's earliest welfare agencies. It grew out of a lavishly furnished barge which docked at the Public Landing so that shiphands could attend church services on a regular basis. Later it helped families in The Basin area who were out of work. The Anna Louise Inn was completed in 1909 and contained 285 rooms. Some of the furnishings were from the city's more historic homes.

THE MAJESTIC CONCERT HALL in 1909 was called one of the Vine Street hotspots—the picture was taken before the spot got hot for the day.

Flood, Freeze, Scandal, and Strike: 1910 to 1920

MORE ANNEXATIONS came early in the decade. West Cumminsville, College Hill, Sayler Park, Carthage, and Madisonville joined the city of Cincinnati. The Reds rebuilt Redland Field, later to be named Crosley Field in honor of Powel Crosley, the radio genius who saved the club from financial collapse. A $2 million fire destroyed much of what was called the shoe district around Ninth and Sycamore.

Fernbank, Hartwell, and Pleasant Ridge joined the city. The Waterworks was built and many were pleased with the water quality. They were not used to such accomplishments from the political machine. The Cincinnati General Hospital opened, and the *New York Times* called it the finest in the entire world.

But 1913 was a year of civic trauma. A flood even greater than that of 1884 brought frothing water higher into the city than ever before. The brand new Waterworks went under, and Cincinnati fought the river until it was back into its banks. Floods had become a tradition, but there had never been one like 1913.

Also in 1913 a streetcar strike shook the city's soggy timbers. Strikebreakers were brought in, and one streetcar was bombarded with bricks and tools and pipe from the huge Union Central Tower, then under construction. After the strike was settled, Cincinnatians bombarded their streetcars with bouquets of flowers in a strange display of civic expiation. The next year the Union Central Building did open and so did the lush, plush Gibson Hotel.

The statues of presidents were on the move in Cincinnati at this time. President Garfield, who had stood in bronze glory in the middle of Eighth and Race Streets, was relocated in Garfield (now Piatt) Park so the motorists wouldn't swear at him any more. In 1917 a statue of Abe Lincoln moved into Lytle Park, still another gift to the city from the Charles P. Taft family.

John Robinson's famous circus was sold in 1916. No more would elephants be common sights in Terrace Park, where Robinson wintered his circus. Each spring the elephants had plowed Robinson's Terrace Park fields, to the consternation of passersby.

In 1917-1918 the river froze solid. In this decade Cleveland became the most populous city in the state, carriage trade declined, and Cincinnati Gas and Electric Company emerged from Cincinnati Gas, Light, and Coke Company.

Carrie Nation inspected the drinking establishments along Vine Street one day and didn't even raise her ax. She hadn't the energy to attack Cincinnati's saloons.

The decade ended with the Reds winning the World Series in the year of the crooked Black Sox Scandal, as the favored White Sox lost. There was also the victorious return of the doughboys who had helped stop the Kaiser. German was no longer taught in Cincinnati's grade schools. Ault Park was donated to the city by Levi A. Ault, and in 1912 a fire demolished the old Gibson House. The Council of Charities and Philanthropies (later the Community Chest) was organized. A tornado struck the Hyde Park area on March 11, 1917. Hamilton County's new courthouse opened in 1919. George B. Cox died in 1916.

[78]

A HISTORIC MOMENT was the unveiling of the statue of William Woodward at Woodward High School in October of 1910. The city's first high school was founded on this same site in 1831. It became Woodward High School and College. An extra floor was added to the structure in 1841. By 1855, a Gothic school replaced the three-story building. In 1910 the new building was dedicated. The school, still functioning, is now Cutter School, named after Woodward's wife, Abigail Cutter. The name Woodward was given to another high school which is on Reading Road at Seymour.

OFFICES SEEMED DARK and murky before fluorescent lighting. This is a scene at Procter & Gamble's general offices around 1910, as accountants and clerks pored over their ledgers. It was about this time that Procter & Gamble acquired its first patents for hydrogenation which resulted in solid vegetable fats or, as it was called when introduced to the world, Crisco.

[79]

THOSE EARLY DRINKING SPOTS weren't all bad. By following the advice on the machine in the back, one could drop a nickel in a slot and hear "a beautiful piano and piccolo duet." This was the Garfield Cafe at Eighth and Vine streets in 1910.

THIS AVID READER would one day be Mayor of Cincinnati, Charles P. Taft. Taft, who lived in the White House while his father, William Howard Taft, was president, was prosecuting attorney of Hamilton County at the age of twenty-nine. He was an original member of the City Charter Committee.

THIS BLACK BEAR was never one of the Cincinnati Zoo's most publicized exhibits because of his drinking habits. He had been captured in the mountains of West Virginia and kept as a pet in a lumber camp, where he acquired his habit at the hands of generous lumbermen. The zoo acquired him and, as the bear grew and became more obstreperous and thirstier, a quart of beer had to be included in his daily ration.

BEFORE RADIO AND TELEVISION newscasters came along, word of elections was available either by telegraph or telephone. Here were some 1913 results coming in over the phone. In other elections, messages would be sent to a crew atop the Union Central Life Insurance Company who flashed a letter or colored light to indicate the victor in certain elections.

A TORNADO touched down briefly in Cincinnati out on Colerain Avenue in 1915, blowing down a building and trapping several of the occupants. During the tornado, a series of fishing camps along the Great Miami blew away, and a steamboat capsized in the Ohio River. In all, 36 died from the storm. In 1917, another one hit Hyde Park, Mount Lookout, and the East End. On May 28, 1809, a tornado stormed through the basin area and petered out on Mount Ida, later known as Mount Adams. The 1840 tornado only hurt crops in Hamilton County, while six persons died during the 1860 twister. The tornados of August 9, 1969, and April 3, 1974, were among the worst in Cincinnati's history.

[81]

GEORGE B. COX *(inset)* died in 1916. The Cox Memorial Theater, built at the start of the 1920s, still stands, mouse gray and rather anonymous, on the north side of Seventh Street between Vine and Walnut streets. The stage of the Cox is now used for storage for the Shubert Theater, on the right. In his later years Boss Cox controlled the World Film Corporation, then the largest movie company in America, and had strong stock positions in the Shubert, Albee, and Keith theater circuits. In 1905 Cox said simply, "I am the Boss of Cincinnati. I've got the best system of government in this country. If I didn't think my system was the best, I would consider that I was a failure in life."

HOSPITALS operated by the Sisters of Charity have been a Cincinnati tradition. Early hospitals were located at Woodward and Broadway and at Third and Plum under the name Saint John's Hotel for Invalids. The nuns took over the United States Marine Hospital at Sixth and Lock in 1866 and called it Good Samaritan. In 1916, patients moved to Clifton Avenue's "Good Sam." The hospital was designed by Gustavew and Drach. Its ecumenical neighbor, immediately to the south, is Hebrew Union College.

BARNEY KROGER'S Sixth Street store did a booming business in 1916. Butchers, off to the left here, didn't have the same refrigeration known today—but that can of baked beans cost nine cents, the corn eight.

SCIONS Julius Fleischmann, son of the founder of the yeast company, and William Cooper Procter, grandson of the co-founder of Procter & Gamble, attended a function in downtown Cincinnati.

DURING THE WINTER of 1917, the Ohio River froze over in spectacular fashion. The winter's freeze saw the adventurous scramble out onto the jagged ice pack that was the river. Later, the river-clogging ice splintered the hulls of steamboats.

THE PARADE on Main Street at the corner of Fifth was interesting for those who were not going off to the First World War but . . .

THE TOWN REALLY WENT WILD when victory was announced at the end of the war. A victory arch was set up on the north side of Fifth Street looking west from Main Street. The inscription read: "Honor For Duty Nobly Done."

Subways and Reform: 1920 to 1930

IT WAS TIME to clean up the city's government. In the election of 1925 the Charter party—a coalition of independent Republicans and Democrats—won control of the city's political life with a home rule charter that made Cincinnati the first major city to adopt a city manager form of government. The city that had been the worst governed purged itself. Murray Seasongood was named mayor. Clean government was here. The first city plan was drawn in 1925.

The decade opened with good news and bad news. The canal was finally drained, and another dimension of Cincinnati life was altered. The canal had played a major role in Cincinnati's development and was one of the keys that unlocked the puzzle of Cincinnati. Uniquely situated, the canal was to become Central Parkway—but not until $6 million had been spent to turn the canal land into that subway.

The river, the single most significant factor in the city's growth and sudden surge to prominence, was channelized by 1929. From Pittsburgh to Cairo, riverboats and barges were guaranteed a nine-foot channel that would keep the river open year-round. The Eden Park obelisk was dedicated to the river in that year by President Herbert Hoover.

The 1920s flappered with joviality. Cincinnati had its prestigious bootlegger, George Remus. The *Island Queen* began her daily trips from the foot of Broadway upriver to Coney Island, running for some twenty-five years before she burned at a mooring in Pittsburgh. The Summer Opera began—at the Zoo of all places. River Downs opened in 1925, only to close down. The Burnet House, once Cincinnati's most illustrious hotel, closed in 1926. Western Hills High School opened, and so did Central Parkway. A year later Bloody Run Boulevard was renamed Victory Parkway, and the gleaming Cincinnati Gas and Electric Company building opened.

The decade closed with the delightful village of Mariemont being dedicated by

Mrs. Thomas Emery. And as they said in *Variety,* "Wall Street laid an egg." Depression was to clutch the country, but Cincinnati fared far better than most other cities. Crosley Radio Corporation (Station WLW) went on the air with what eventually became the most powerful transmitter in the world. Four steamers burned at wharfside. U.C.'s James G. Nippert Stadium was completed in 1924. Mr. and Mrs. Charles P. Taft offered their home as a museum through the Institute of Fine Arts.

THE KNIGHTS OF COLUMBUS paraded on November 16, 1920, from Eighth Street and Sunset Avenue to celebrate the laying of the cornerstone of the Saint William's Church on Price's Hill.

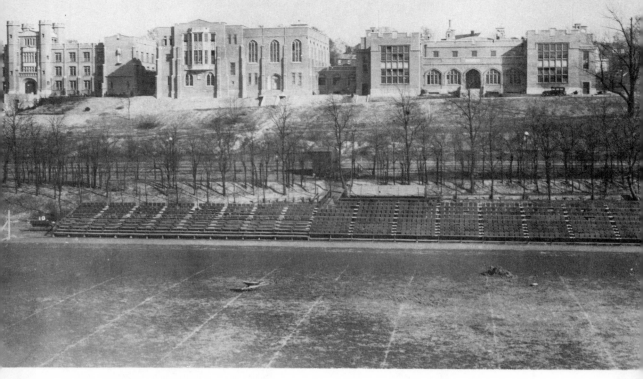

THE SAINT XAVIER COLLEGE campus sprouted above Bloody Run in 1920. The Evanston school looked out over the makeshift football stadium before Corcoran Field was built in 1928 at a cost of $300,000. The university stands on the grounds of the old Avondale Athletic Club.

EVEN BEFORE THERE WAS OPERA at the Cincinnati Zoo, there was this handsome pavilion. The basic stage remained the same when a covering was constructed for the audience.

CINCINNATI'S brand new Grisard Field *(above)* was dedicated on September 5, 1922. The field was in Blue Ash and was given serious consideration as the site of a major air terminal in the 1940s before the airport in Kentucky was approved.

THE FIRST AIRMAIL *(below)* was brought by a plane on August 5, 1922, at Grisard Field. The field's name was later changed to Watson Field.

PEEBLES CORNER *(below)* had grown beyond James Kemper's expectations when this aerial photo was taken, probably in the early 1920s. Kemper was Cincinnati's first Presbyterian minister who bought 130 acres of walnut-treed hills from John Cleves Symmes. Kemper donated sixty acres to Lane Seminary on the east side of Gilbert, north of Yale. The seminary was torn down in 1932. The home of Dr. Lyman Beecher, seminary head, is maintained as a museum and called The Harriet Beecher Stowe House.

EVEN THOUGH the main branch of the library downtown was operating out of an antiquated building in the 1920s, everything was up to date with the bookmobile which, though smaller than today's, got books out to the people.

THE PLACE TO LOOK AT FLOWERS in 1924 was the Eden Park Green House, which preceded the Krohn Conservatory.

POWEL CROSLEY put his pioneer radio station on the air in 1922. The 500-watt station became the most powerful in the nation when it broadcast from its Mason, Ohio, transmitter with 500,000 watts. Crosley got into the radio business when his son asked for a radio. Crosley was so surprised at the cost that he built one for his son.

WHEN WSAI first went on the air (without Jim Scott), it was owned by the U.S. Playing Card Company on Beech Street in Norwood. In 1885, the U.S. Playing Card Company introduced its Bicycle brand, famed in legend and gambling casinos around the world. U.S. Playing Card is the largest producer of cards in the country.

FOUR DISTINGUISHED SONS of the late Alphonso Taft were photographed together on November 2, 1925, at the dedication of the Alphonso Taft Law College at the University of Cincinnati. From the left: New York attorney Henry W. Taft, Chief Justice William Howard Taft, Cincinnati newspaper owner Charles P. Taft, and Forrest D. Taft, head master of the Taft School at Watertown, Connecticut.

COL. CLARENCE O. SHERRILL was plucked from Washington to be the first city manager under the city's new governmental structure in 1925. Sherrill, formerly military aide to President Harding, was responsible for construction of the Lincoln Memorial and the $15 million memorial bridge between Washington, D. C. and Arlington, Virginia. Sherrill served for five years before becoming a vice-president of the Kroger Grocery and Baking Company in 1930. He resumed city manager duties following the 1937 flood.

TWO OF CINCINNATI'S most prominent and generous citizens were Charles P. Taft *(below left)* and Anna Sinton Taft, his spouse. Charles P. Taft preferred newspapers to legal reference works. He bought the *Cincinnati Times* in 1879 to become its editor and publisher, and added the *Star* in 1880 to make it the *Cincinnati Times-Star.* He also was owner of the German-language newspaper *Volksblatt.* The Tafts did much for the city. They were active with the May Festival, supported the Symphony, the Zoo, and the Zoo Opera. Since their two daughters were adequately provided for, the Tafts gave the city their home, their art collection, and $2,700,000 in cash in 1932. After their marriage, the Tafts moved in with David Sinton, her father, the hotel man whose handsome hotel at Fourth and Vine has been replaced by the Provident Bank Building. Sinton had made much of his money in the iron foundry business prior to and during the Civil War. He was an authentic Cincinnati character, blunt in speech, careless in dress, and a disarming penny-pincher.

MRS. MARY EMERY, clutching the shovel and bouquet, celebrated the first anniversary of Marie-mont. John R. Schindel, Thomas Hogan, Jr. and Rev. Frank Nelson looked on. Mrs. Emery conceived the model town that would meet her ideals of careful city planning. John Nolen, a town planner, laid out the 420 acres of farmland she acquired and constructed the little village from scratch. Designed primarily as a residential district for wage earners of different economic grades, the village would surround the town center which provided for every sort of building: shops, markets, a theater, hotel, office buildings, playgrounds, and a village green.

GEORGE REMUS sold $75 million worth of liquor in a two-year period. At the same time, he is said to have spent $20 million paying off various federal, state, and local law enforcement officers for their silence. Remus, Cincinnati's most famous boot-legger, was finally convicted and sent to an Atlanta penitentiary; his wife filed for divorce just prior to his release. An attorney, he fought the divorce proceedings with such vigor that it was two years before it was scheduled for a court hearing. Two hours before court convened, Remus caught his wife in Eden Park and shot and killed her. His plea of temporary insanity kept him from jail, and three months later he was back in Cincinnati. Remus is pictured here with his daughter at the murder trial.

THESE THREE HOUSES stood on the present site of the Ohio National Life Insurance Company at the corner of William Howard Taft Road and Highland Avenue. Miss Bertha Pfirman, who lived in the middle house, later had the corner house torn down, and turned the middle house ninety degrees.

BURNET HOUSE finally came down, to be supplanted by the Union Central Annex, on January 17, 1926. Several of Judge Jacob Burnet's descendants took part in the ceremonies.

CINCINNATI'S NEW MAYOR, Murray Seasongood, left, attended a college graduation at the University of Cincinnati with U.C. President Frederick C. Hicks. Seasongood, a Cincinnati native, graduated from Woodward High School and Harvard Law School. He was the city's first mayor under the city charter, serving from 1926 to 1930. He laid the groundwork toward the drafting of the new charter of 1924. He has been president of the Hamilton County Good Government League, and President of the National Association of the Legal Aid Organization.

A DOCTOR AND NURSE at the Community Chest Building performed dental work for those who needed it in 1927.

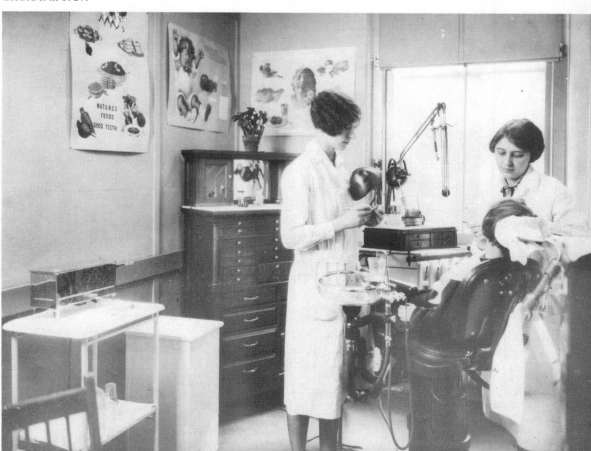

TRAFFIC WAS TWO-WAY on all downtown streets in 1927. Mabley and Carew was on the northeast corner of Fifth and Vine. In a couple of years it would go to the southwest corner before moving to the northwest corner where it is today, the first building on the left in this picture. The original Mabley's site became part of the new Fountain Square Plaza in the 1970s.

PRESIDENT HOOVER came here on October 23, 1929, to dedicate the nine-foot channelization of
the Ohio River from Pittsburgh to Cairo, Illinois. The obelisk *(above)* is in Eden Park and marks the
halfway point of the river. President Hoover had made the trip from Pittsburgh by steamboat, and
some twenty steamboats which accompanied him tied up at the again bustling riverfront *(below)*.

WHILE CHESTER PARK'S star was beginning to fade toward the end of the 1920s *(above)*, the meticulously kept Coney Island *(left)* attracted more and more summer visitors. The park was noted for the absence of litter and its overall cleanliness. The *Island Queen* took excursionists up-river three time a day.

THE TAWDRY Miami-Erie Canal was finally drained, and work started on a subway system *(above)* which turned out to be a political boondoggle. The $6-million Underground Rapid Transit had a station, too, at Canal and Race streets *(right)*, which was as deserted as the entire subway is to this day. But a bright and shiny Central Parkway *(below)*, newly landscaped, supplanted the canal and contributed to better traffic in the city, hiding the useless subway.

THE ENTIRE WESTERN HILLS AREA was apt to be shut off from the rest of the city if there were a flood along the Mill Creek. After years of planning and fighting, the Western Hills Viaduct went under construction in the late 1920s and was formally dedicated in 1933.

[100]

BRIGHTON, called the key to Western Hills, was a traffic jam waiting to happen in the late 1920s. In the right background workmen labor over Central Parkway.

Just Making It: 1930 to 1940

THE DECADE BEGAN with heavy construction. The Carew Tower bricks were laid up almost overnight. The Art Museum got additional space, and Suzie the Gorilla came to live at the Zoo. Following restoration, Taft Museum was opened to the public.

And in 1933, at about the time the feasibility of flight was being proved, Union Terminal opened. You could drive across the new double-deck Western Hills Viaduct and look out over the new railroad terminal, undoubtedly the finest in the land, and its half-rotunda. Eugene Goossens came to conduct the Cincinnati Symphony, and the Spencer House on Front and Broadway was torn down. Guests at Spencer House before its decline had included President Andrew Johnson, Generals Grant and Custer, and even Jean Jacques Rousseau.

The new post office opened its doors in 1939, and Columbia Parkway was built as a WPA project. Laurel—Richmond housing project near the terminal opened with room for 1,303 families. Roselawn joined the city. Barney Kroger, the extraordinary grocer who started his career with a handcart, died, and so did William Howard Taft. The Reds made more history. The first big league night baseball game was played here in 1935. Johnny VanderMeer pitched two no-hitters—in a row! And the Reds won the National League pennant in 1939. Fortunately Prohibition was over and Cincinnatians could celebrate with elan.

Even though depression stalked the streets of Cincinnati, the industrial base was diversified enough. Things were better here than in most places. Often they are.

But the river was still a force not to be forgotten. In January 1937 flood waters rose to 80 feet, the highest ever. Rampaging waters swirled up the Mill Creek, and even Knowlton's Corner was awash. Gas from a storage tank spilled out onto the angry waters; a spark and disaster! Firemen fought in water up to their necks through the night and into the next day until the fire was finally controlled. During the night gas tanks exploded, spewing more fuel onto the water that famed Black Sunday, January 24, 1937. Before the flood was over, Cincinnatians were getting food and water from out of town or from generous neighbors in Norwood and other places with independent water supplies.

THIS HOLE IN THE GROUND would some day be the basement of the Carew Tower, Cincinnati's tallest building. The tower, 574 feet above street level, was completed in 1930. The building, designed to hold a hotel and two department stores, is capped by an observation deck which provides one of the best views of the area.

THERE WAS ONLY ONE SUZIE! She came to America aboard the *Graf Zeppelin* in 1929 and was the only trained gorilla in America. Children from around the area queued up to see Susie feed herself with fork and spoon and brush her teeth. She ate with utensils only when her trainer, William Dressman, ate at the same table. She would always offer Dressman a bite of whatever morsel she was having for lunch in her four-room apartment at the zoo. She died October 30, 1947.

LUNKEN AIRPORT was the commercial airport for Cincinnati for many years. It had been given by E. H. Lunken to a private company which eventually turned the field over to the City of Cincinnati. The airport was dedicated in September of 1930 and was served by Mason Dixon Airlines, Embry-Riddle Airline, and Universal Aviation Corporation.

AUGUST HERRMANN, head of the Cincinnati Waterworks, owner of the Cincinnati Reds, associate of Cox and Hynicka, died in 1931. He has been called the "Father of the World Series," was the equivalent to the commissioner of baseball before the 1919 Black Sox Scandal, and Grand Exalted Ruler of All the Elks in America. Herrmann managed to keep much of the taint of the Cox machine away from his own life.

WALNUT HILLS HIGH SCHOOL, since its completion in 1931, has been one of the city's more handsome buildings. The thirty-three-acre campus and the neo-Georgian architecture command a splendid view of Victory Parkway.

WHILE DRAFTSMEN WORKED in their offices in the Temple Bar Building in 1928 . . .

WORKMEN WERE BUSY stripping the knob off Bald Knob for fill dirt behind the . . .

UNION TERMINAL which was beginning to take shape as a rather spiffy train station. This picture was taken in March of 1932.

TROLLEY CARS still rattled around Fountain Square when the Cincinnati Public Works Department took this photo on April 1, 1932. The old Federal Building and Post Office, upper left, had not yet been razed to make way for the present-day structure. The huge advertising sign atop the building at the southeast corner of Fifth and Main (upper center) proclaims the merits of a tonic marketed by Gilbert Mosby, who was referred to as the Konjola King. His comparatively brief financial success included residence in an eastern Cincinnati mansion where there were said to be gold-plated bathroom fixtures.

THE SHILLITO MANSION in Mount
Auburn at Highland Avenue and Oak
Street became the College-Conservatory
of Music. When CCM became the four-
teenth college at the University of Cincinnati in the early 1960s, the building
was razed to make way for a junior high
school.

THE INDIAN HILL RANGERS served
for many years on one of the few pri-
vately supported police forces in the
area. Indian Hill residents paid directly
for their protection. The well-equipped
Rangers were among the first to have
two-way radio communication.

IN 1935, the Cincinnati brain trust
looked over its prospects for the coming
year. Observers Larry MacPhail, Charley
Dressen, and Powel Crosley confer during
a visit to the spring training site in Tampa.

THE BLACK SUNDAY FIRE at Crosley
Radio and the Standard Oil storage
station in January 1937 lasted for 12
hours in Camp Washington. Loss of $1.5
million was estimated for the fire which
burned over a three and a half square
mile area.

CINCINNATI IS A CHILI KIND of a
place in many ways (well, at least three-
ways) more than Texas is. Here is one of
the city's earliest and best–the Empress
Chili Parlor which took its name from
the burlesk next door. Later the burlesk
was changed to burlesque, and the theater was renamed the Gayety.

BEECHMONT LEVEE gave way during the 1937 flood, the worst one in Cincinnati's recorded history, and a 50-foot section tumbled down into Lunken Airport Playfield. (Perhaps this was when "Sunken Lunken" got its name.) Before the 1937 flood was finished, more than 100,000 people in Greater Cincinnati had been driven from their homes, about one-sixth of Cincinnati was under water, and property damage was estimated at $25,000,000–and those were Depression dollars.

THE FOOT OF BROADWAY kept going higher and higher during the 1937 flood. The river crested at 80 feet, but before it receded, the flood ravaged much of Cincinnati's low land.

THE EXPANDING UNIVERSITY OF CINCINNATI got its Student Union in 1937.

ANNA MARIE HAHN was the first woman to die in Ohio's electric chair. Mrs. Hahn was accused of murdering five persons. She was discovered after her son, Oscar, found a small bottle of oily medicine behind the sofa in their home. Police, who had been investigating the murders of the five, were called in, arrested and charged Mrs. Hahn. Here, moments after being found guilty of murder in the poison death of Jacob Wagner, Mrs. Hahn, a former German housemaid, was accompanied to her cell. Her defense attorney was Hiram Bolesinger, Sr.

CINCINNATIANS WENT TO SEE how well the government did when it built public housing. Laurel-Richmond Homes, the Federal West End Housing Project, was inspected during its inaugural open house in June 1938.

CINCINNATIANS in the Ohio National Guard watered horses after a tough day of maneuvers at Camp Perry in summer of 1938.

THE GEORGE PENDLETON HOUSE, at the corner of Liberty and Highland, looked like a tenement house in January 1938. The building was completely refurbished in the 1960s and is of great historic interest. It was here that Sen. George Pendleton wrote the Pendleton, or Civil Service, Act—the first law that covered employment practices by the Federal Government. The act was passed in 1883.

INDIANA LIMESTONE handsomely filled in the new Cincinnati Post Office on Fifth between Main and Walnut in early 1938. The city's first post office was established in 1793, and Abner M. Dunn was the first postmaster. The post office has been housed in seven buildings since its establishment. It stood for nearly thirty years at Fourth and Vine streets where Central Trust Tower is today.

JOHNNY VANDERMEER did the impossible on June 11 and 15, 1938. VanderMeer pitched two consecutive no-hitters against the Boston Braves and the Brooklyn Dodgers. The feat has never been duplicated.

ALL THE WORLD LOVES A WINNER, and the Reds were winners of the National League Championship in 1939. It was the first such celebration since the 1919 Black Sox Scandal.

THE NEWLY OPENED AULT PARK looked like a geometric exercise in the late 1930s. The park was named after Mr. and Mrs. Levi Addison Ault who donated all but thirty acres of the 235-acre park to the city. The park is in Mount Lookout. Ault was the first president of Cincinnati's modern Park Board, serving from 1908 to 1926. Cincinnati has more than eighty-five parks on 3,650 acres.

EVEN DURING THE DEPTHS OF THE DEPRESSION, a ride on the *Island Queen* guaranteed a lift of spirits, as it cruised the Ohio on the way to and from Coney Island. Big bands played when the boat rides began in early spring, before Coney Island opened. Clyde Trask kicked off the 1939 sailing season.

CINCINNATI'S SAFETY LANE was dedicated in January 1940 to the beat of a uniformed band. Cincinnatians are expected to have their autos inspected each year.

UNION TERMINAL broke out the bunting *(left)* to welcome the Reds back from a profitable 1940 road trip. The Reds had taken 10 of 16 games on the trip, and went on to win the National League pennant and the World Series. But not everyone seemed to think the civic exuberance was fun *(below)*.

A Crown Askew: 1940 to 1950

THE REDS WON the National League pennant again in 1940 and went on to win the World Series. The international situation was on everyone's mind, and soon Cincinnatians were off to fight in World War II. As the GIs were leaving, Chester Park was closing down. Garfield Park was renamed Piatt Park, after the brothers who gave it to the city, and the National Theater at Third and Sycamore was torn down. It had been nothing more than a tobacco warehouse in its late years. English Woods opened.

During the war, a board of Kentuckians from Kenton County finished building an airport in Boone County, Kentucky, named the new facility after Cincinnati, and watched porters put "CVG" on luggage—and that stands for Covington. Geographically confused as it was, the Greater Cincinnati Airport would thrive in the virgin land of Boone County.

Meanwhile the 1948 Master Plan was unveiled; it called for a highway distributor along Third Street and even a stadium on the Riverfront. Station WLWT got into the television business in 1948, and the Public Library wanted to move to a new building at Eighth and Vine. While some were dreaming of a stadium on the river, an arena, Cincinnati Gardens, was erected near Swifton Village.

The Emery interests designed and built a startling hotel, first known as the Terrace Plaza, Sixth and Vine streets. *Time* magazine took one look at the new building and said it was dandy but Cincinnati was "dowdy." The citizens were upset at that, but if they looked around, they saw what they had let Cincinnati become. The Queen's crown truly was a little tarnished, perhaps even askew. Perhaps something could be done. Perhaps.

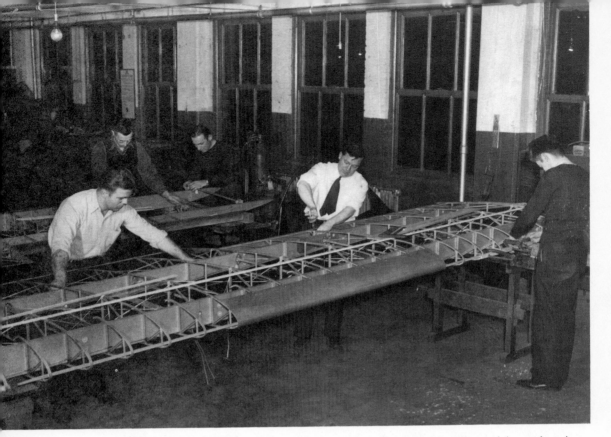

THE AVIATION HIGH SCHOOL at the corner of Seventh and Broadway was training students in early 1941 for skills in which employment prospects were high.

CINCINNATI'S MACHINE TOOL INDUSTRIES geared up at the start of World War II to make the machines that helped win the war. The name "Cincinnati" was so prevalent on certain machine tools that, for a period of time, machine tools in Russia were known as "Cincinnatis."

YOU CAN TAKE the politician out of the country, but you can't take the politicians out of the Carthage Fair. Former Gov. Myers Y. Cooper (left), president of the Carthage Fair Board for many years, opened the 1941 fair with Mayor James G. Stewart. The first Ohio agriculture society was formed in Cincinnati in 1819 with Gen. William Henry Harrison as president, and the first fair with prizes was held in 1820. The Carthage Fair itself originated in 1846, and the present fairgrounds were acquired in 1847. Ohio's first state fair was held in Cincinnati in 1850.

FINDLAY MARKET is in itself a 125-year tradition. It is involved in another tradition, opening day ceremonies with the Reds. Manager Bill McKechnie received a 1941 plaque, celebrating the Reds' World Championship, from Fred L. Emmert to the right of the plaque. Findlay Market, known throughout the area for its grocery and butcher stalls, just completed a refurbishing. The market was named for Gen. James Findlay who owned much of the real estate in the area around the 1830s. Executors of Findlay's estate gave the Findlay Market space to the City of Cincinnati in 1852. Old Cincinnati families have shopped and operated stands at the market for many generations.

[119]

CINCINNATI at her absolute "serenest," in the mid-1940s. This photograph was regarded as the portrait of the town for many years.

ROOKWOOD POTTERY, at the start of the 1940s, was internationally known for its jewel porcelain pottery. The pottery was founded in 1880 by Mrs. Maria Longworth Storer who named it Rookwood after her father's country estate off Edwards and Grandin roads. The present Rookwood buildings were erected in 1892 and expanded in 1899 and 1904. The pottery has long since ceased operation, though the kilns still stand. Sales staff admire the work in the above picture.

THERE WERE FEW THINGS more complicated than counting a proportional representation ballot in Cincinnati. First all the ballots were counted to determine the total valid votes. Invalid ballots were discarded. To be elected, a candidate had to poll one-tenth of the total vote plus one. If, for example, the total vote was 100,000, a candidate's quota was 10,001. When he got that many, he was declared elected. All of the first choice votes—those designated as No.1—were counted. Then, the extra votes a winning candidate received were distributed to the candidates marked number two on those ballots. Later, as the race tightened, third and fourth choices would be used until all nine members of council were elected. Here is the 1941 election count at the Hotel Gibson.

EUGENE GOOSSENS prepared to conduct the Cincinnati Symphony Orchestra before a full house in 1941. Goossens had succeeded Fritz Reiner ten years earlier. During the Depression the Cincinnati Symphony's grave economic problems were solved by the Cincinnati Institute of Fine Arts funded by the Charles P. Tafts in 1927.

THE POLICE DEPARTMENT went to two-way radio communication with the radio dispatch office in 1942. The office, called Station X, was considered one of the most modern of the time.

DURING THE WAR, scrap metal was sought from every possible source. The John Shillito Company dismantled its marquee at Shillito Place for the steel during a 1942 scrap metal drive. The company first moved to its present location in 1877.

L. B. WILSON (left), a broadcasting genius, was the power behind WCKY's success. The station's country music format was heard throughout the Southeast, where programs were beamed with special intensity. Here he is receiving a Red Cross award from Dr. Carl Wilzbach for acquiring 1486 blood donors during World War II.

RIVER DOWNS (the old Coney Island Race Track) was a picture of calm as the fourth race was about to get underway on September 8, 1943. The race track opened in 1925, and operated on and off until 1937 when it had to be rebuilt after the flood.

AN ENTHUSIASTIC CROWD gathered in Fountain Square on V-E Day, May 20, 1945.

AT LAST! The war was over after Japan surrendered. Pandemonium reigned delightfully in front of the Albee Theater on Fountain Square.

EVEN THOUGH THE WAR WAS OVER, the Union Terminal concourse didn't show it at Christmas 1945. Thousands of soldiers passed through the terminal in one of its busiest seasons.

THE EARLY DAYS of WCPO-TV were noted for their creative nonsense. These were four clowns from the Symmes Street Studios: (clockwise from top left) Len Goorian, Dotty Mack, Paul Dixon, and Wanda Lewis.

UNDOUBTEDLY THE BEST DRESSED REPORTER in 1946, Al Schottelkotte *(left)* was also one of the city's youngest. He started work as a copy clerk at the *Cincinnati Enquirer* in March 1943, when he was sixteen years old and still a student at Saint Xavier High School. He became a reporter three months later. One of his early assignments was covering a story of five men accused of attacking a woman in a Newport park, but those under twenty-one were barred from the courtroom. The clerk felt he had to run out the sixteen-year-old Schottelkotte who did some fast talking, as he does now as Cincinnati's top-rated newscaster, and continued to cover the trial—inside.

FRANK WEIKEL *(right),* a chubby-cheeked Purcell High School graduate, had just been promoted on the *Enquirer* staff to police reporter, while Josiah Cornell *(below right),* no-nonsense reporter for the *Cincinnati Post,* was getting his career in high gear. Another one just getting started at mid-century was Bob Braun *(left),* the Ludlow, Kentuckian who sang for Mutual Broadcasting. Braun began his Cincinnati broadcasting career with WCPO-TV, and later went to WLW as a disc jockey and movie host. He replaced Ruth Lyons on the 50-50 Club when she retired.

THE CINCINNATI & SUBURBAN Bell Telephone Company's straight-line toll switchboard, the world's longest, was lonely and nearly deserted during a 1946 strike. The switchboard, 166 feet long, had 88 operator positions. The company was founded by Andrew Erkenbrecher, founder of the Cincinnati Zoological Gardens.

BUSINESS DOWNTOWN was described as brisk this pre-Christmas shopping day in 1946. Fifth and Vine's sidewalks overflowed out onto the streets.

GEORGE RATTERMAN played his high school basketball at Saint Xavier and was voted the best basketball player in a Madison Square Garden tournament. He often backed up quarterback Johnny Lujack at Notre Dame, and later was the All-America Football Conference's 1947 Rookie of the Year as quarterback for the Buffalo Bills. He was best known, however, as the backup quarterback for the Cleveland Browns behind Otto Graham. Ratterman went on to escape a lurid frameup and became the reform sheriff of Campbell County, Kentucky.

THE WIFE of Cincinnati Manager W. R. Kellogg brandished a bottle of Chianti as she baptized the "Cincinnatian" train which ran between Cincinnati and Washington, D. C. The train got on the track in January of 1947.

OPENING DAY for the Cincinnati Reds is something of a tradition. Businessmen leave their desks, students cut classes and throng to the ballpark. This full house at Crosley Field was the start of the 1948 season.

THIS YOUNG EASTERN LEAGUE BASEBALL UMpire went on to put the University of Cincinnati on the basketball map. John "Socko" Wiethe, who was once considered too light to play at Roger Bacon High School, went on to a distinguished collegiate and professional football career before becoming head basketball coach at U. C. Later, lawyer-coach Wiethe settled into politics and enjoyed a colorful career as a Democratic chieftain.

FOR MANY YEARS, Cincinnati's streetcars looked like these waiting outside Crosley Field for an after-game crowd. On Sundays anyone could buy a pass that gave him unlimited rides all that day on Cincinnati streetcars. It was an easy, day-killing way to see all the sights of the town.

ONE OF THE MOST SUCCESSFUL FOOTBALL coaches of the University of Cincinnati was Sid Gillman, a former Miami and West Point coach who joined the University of Cincinnati in 1948. Gillman managed to get the U.C. Bearcats into the national Top 20s during the 1950s, and had the Reed Shank Memorial Pavillion added to Nippert Stadium to handle the standing-room-only crowds during his tenure. Gillman left Cincinnati to coach the Los Angeles Rams, then the San Diego Chargers, and the Houston Oilers.

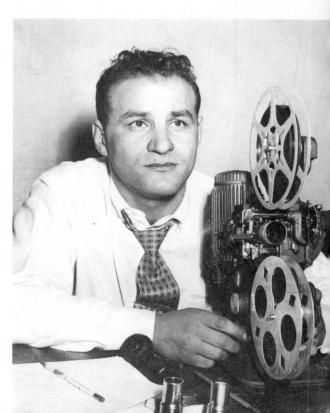

NATHAN L. COMISAR *(right)*, a Russian native, came to Cincinnati when he was thirteen years old, and eventually owned LaNormandie-Maisonette on Walnut between Fifth and Sixth streets. In the late 1940s, he began the transformation that saw the Maisonette become one of the nation's most honored restaurants. Today the Maisonette, named by Comisar after the old Maisonette Room in New York's St. Regis Hotel, is the annual recipient of the significant good dining awards. Pictured above is the old Maisonette as it began its changeover to elegance. At this time, the floors are not carpeted, and coat hooks dot the pillars.

DAN TEHAN, a politician and National Football League official, began in 1949 a crackdown on Hamilton County gamblers that spread his name across the state. He obtained a Ph.D. from Xavier University in 1928, and officiated in the American Association and the Southern Conference. He was elected Hamilton County Sheriff in 1948 in his first venture into politics.

ROBERT A. TAFT, brother of Charles, son of William Howard, and father of Robert, Jr., was one of the most illustrious of an illustrious clan. Taft was born here in 1889. He ranked at the head of his class when he graduated from Yale in 1910 and led his Harvard Law School class in 1913. Taft served as State Representative in 1920 and was Speaker of the House in 1926. In 1940, as U. S. Senator from Ohio, Taft sought the presidential nomination. His wife Martha gave him a kiss good-bye as he launched the push. In 1948, Taft again battled for the Republican presidential nomination only to lose to New York's Thomas E. Dewey *(below)*. Taft's loss to Eisenhower for the nomination in 1952 occurred just a year before his death. His Taft-Hartley Act, passed over a Harry S. Truman veto, was one of his significant legislative acts.

[133]

AL LEWIS began as an off-the-air artist and on-the-air song and dance man. In 1950, he and his wife Wanda took those first tentative steps towards TV stardom—Cincinnati style. In an early show, trying to kill time, Lewis talked to a couple of neighborhood kids who wandered into the studio. TV was like that in the early WCPO days. His boss, Mortimer C. Watters, saw the episode and knew he had a winner. Thus Uncle Al and Captain Wendy were born, and twenty-five years later still babysit for Cincinnati's children.

WLW WAS GOING into the television business on Mount Olympus in November 1947. The station was testing equipment and a number of broadcast firsts occurred around this time. The first TV picture in Cincinnati was on June 4, 1946, when W8XCT was testing at Carew Tower. The first regular program was on July 31, 1947 at 8:30 p.m. The first baseball game televised was the Reds vs. the Phillies on September 21, 1947. The first wrestling match faked its way onto the screens four days later. The first football game was U.C. vs. Dayton on October 11, 1947, and the first basketball game was U.C. vs. Kentucky on December 13. Wiedemann Brewery had the first commercial on February 2, 1948, and Cincinnati's life hasn't been the same since.

THERE WERE LOTS OF CHANCES involved in walking out onto the iced-over Ohio River. Police kept chasing poeple off the ice at Anderson Ferry, but as soon as the police departed, people scrambled back onto the floes. This was in February 1948.

THE TERRACE PLAZA was under construction in 1947. It was the first step in the city's long road back to vitality and quality. The hotel was considered such an architectural achievement that the American Institute of Architects devoted ten pages in its publication to a discussion of the ultra-modern building. The hotel, now the Terrace Hilton. featured a lobby and an ice skating rink on the eighth floor. The rounded edge, top center, is the home of the award-winning Gourmet Room. The hotel replaced the Greenwood Building on the southwest corner of Sixth and Vine which was, for more than sixty years, the home of the Ohio Mechanics Institute. The building was named after Miles Greenwood, one of Cincinnati's early industrialists and promoter of Cincinnati's first paid fire department. However, it was called the "Fire Tower" because a fire watch was maintained from its roof. The Terrace Plaza also replaced the Oxford Hotel at the corner of Sixth and Race. The Oxford had enjoyed a long and respectable, though not distinguished, career.

CINCINNATI HAS HAD a development plan ever since 1925. In 1948 Sherwood Ruder, director of the Master Plan study, presented the plan to officials of surrounding communities. The Master Plan called for a riverfront stadium, arena, and the Third Street Distributor or Fort Washington Way. The 1925 plan had called for widening Columbia Parkway, immediate creation of Duck Creek Parkway, abandoning of Anderson Ferry School, abandoning of the library on Vine Street, and cooperation in the building of a "union passenger station."

[135]

IF SHE CHIDED, you listened. Ruth Lyons was the most powerful woman in Cincinnati during the 1950s and 1960s. Ruth Lyons began her career as a pianist on WKRC radio in 1929. By 1933, she had ad-libbed her way onto the air and was named program director. In 1942, three years after the Ruth Lyons Christmas Fund was started, she joined WLW. In 1946 her "50 Club" made its radio debut, followed by TV in 1949. She retired in 1967. Her Christmas Fund is one of Cincinnati's exceptional philanthropies and has been perpetuated by Bob Braun who followed her on the "50-50 Club."

GREATER CINCINNATI AIRPORT launched the boom in Boone County in the late 1940s. This picture shows the original buildings at the airport before any expansion. The field, runways, and taxi-strip were completed by August of 1944. Formal dedication of the Boone County airport and its terminal building was on October 27, 1947. It should be noted that before work could begin on the airport, federal agents confiscated a 160-gallon still, 400 gallons of mash, and some barrels. That's how far out Boone County was in those days.

THE DREAM OF A SMALL CAR with low gas consumption was
Powel Crosley, Jr.'s. It was a dream fifteen years too soon. Here's
Crosley with the light engine to his inimitable "Crosley."

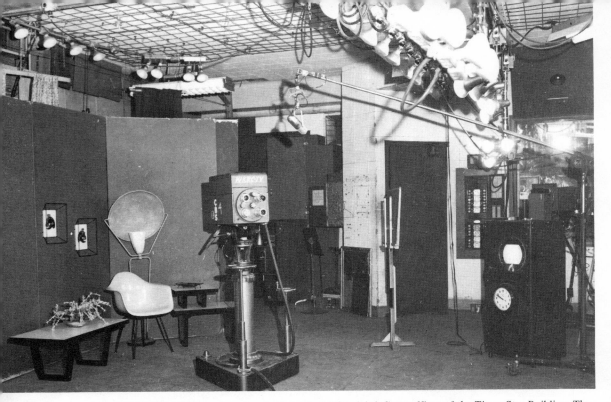

WHEN WKRC-TV went on the air, it was from the eighth-floor offices of the Times-Star Building. The studios were cramped and low-ceilinged, forcing the move to the present Mount Auburn location. The late night newscaster on WKRC-TV around this time? Stan Matlock.

JUST BEFORE THE LIBRARY moved to Eighth and Vine streets, it still managed to look like it could have been an opera house. The library was little more than a four-story auditorium with an open well from the first to the fourth floors. Each of the nooks off to the side of the well was filled with books, and it was a common sight to see young library employees scramble among the stacks like trained chimps. Originally, the building was designed by James McLaughlin for Truman Handy and was known as The Handy Opera House, though not a note was ever sung there. Instead it became the library.

Cincinnati Since 1950

CINCINNATI SNOOZED FITFULLY through the fifties. The *Time* jibe calling the town "dowdy" was hard to swallow, but it was managed without a discernible gulp. Downtown decayed. No bridges had been built across the River since the automobile was invented. But the town's sinew hadn't turned to flab. The city's industrial arm flexed mightily as ever. Cincinnati would never boom again, it would never bust either.

Cincinnati had awakened from her sleep well-rested; there was still work to do, quality to keep, renown to recapture. Though there was a different drummer, the beat was sure, the beat was steady. The queen was coming back.

Once the city had been saved from too rapid a growth rate by its ring of unscalable hills. And it escaped helter-skelter renewal.

Planners, developers, cranes, and common sense transfigured downtown. Office hovels fell before the bulldozer's blade. Empty stores vanished before the wrecker's ball. Renaissance! A downtown built for people, safe for people, enjoyed by people. A resplendent home for the fountain gleamed. The stadium sprouted on the riverfront, and the Bengals were born. Where steamboats had put in, a hockey arena arose.

The city's strong heart pumped vitality through the region. Quiet, undiscovered Cincinnati had not overgrown. It was too big to be small town, too small to be a big town. It was the best of both: you can stand on the corner of Sixth and Vine and "know" people who walk past; you can lose yourself among 50,000 fans at Riverfront Stadium.

The Christian Science Monitor has found Cincinnati to be "one of the country's 10 most livable cities." Most of us knew that all along.

BIBLIOGRAPHY

Cist, Charles, *Cincinnati in 1841, etc.*, Cincinnati, 1841.

Cist, Charles, *Sketches and Statistics of Cincinnati in 1851,* Cincinnati, 1851.

De Chambrun, Clara, Countess, *Cincinnati; Story of the Queen City,* New York, 1939.

Dickens, Charles, *American Notes,* London, 1842.

Goss, Charles, Frederick, *Cincinnati, the Queen City 1788-1924,* 4 vols., Chicago and Cincinnati, 1912.

Hessler, Iola O., *Cincinnati Then And Now,* Cincinnati, 1949.

Kenny, D. J., *Illustrated Guide to Cincinnati,* Cincinnati, 1893.

Morsbach, Mabel, *We Live In Cincinnati,* Cincinnati, 1961.

Ohio Writers' Project, WPA, *Cincinnati Guide,* Cincinnati, 1943.

Perry, Dick, *Vas You Ever in Zinzinnati?.* Garden City, 1966.

Williams, Caroline, *The City On Seven Hills,* Cincinnati, 1938.

Index of Names